DIARY OF A BEATLEMANIAC

DIARY OF A BEATLEMANIAC

A Fab Insider's Look at the Beatles Era

PATRICIA GALLO-STENMAN
WITH A FOREWORD BY LARRY KANE

CYNREN PRESS

Malvern, Pennsylvania

PUBLISHED BY CYNREN PRESS

101 Lindenwood Drive, Suite 225

Malvern, PA 19355 USA

http://www.cynren.com/

⎯⎯⎯

PRINTED IN THE UNITED STATES OF AMERICA ON ACID-FREE PAPER

ISBN-13: 978-1-947976-03-0 (pbk)

ISBN-13: 978-1-947976-04-7 (ebk)

Library of Congress Control Number: 2017964647

Every effort has been made to trace the ownership of copyrighted material. Information that will enable the publisher to rectify any error or omission in subsequent reprints will be welcome. In such cases, please contact the publisher at press@cynren.com.

All photographs are taken by or from the collection of Patricia Gallo-Stenman © 2018, except where noted. Author photograph by Crystal Wood.

To maintain their anonymity, in some instances, names of individuals have been changed.

Teen Scene, "Review of the Beatles," "Beatle's Buddy Gives Gals Wrap," and "I Love the Beatles Essay Contest" articles are used with permission of Philadelphia Daily News © 2013. All rights reserved.

Teen to Teen articles are used with permission of the *Globe Times*.

Cover photograph reproduced with special permission from the Special Collections Research Center, Temple University Libraries, Philadelphia, PA. Photograph by Sam Nocella. Photograph has been cropped.

BOOK DESIGN by The Frontispiece

In loving memory of John and Jennie Gallo

Omnia vincit amor

—VIRGIL, ECLOGUE X

CONTENTS

ACKNOWLEDGMENTS

Many individuals assisted me down this "long and winding road": Robin Bartlett, who pushed, prodded, and pulled me through the project to the finish line and whose professionalism and steady guidance greatly encouraged me; publisher Holly Monteith, who believed in what Patti had to say; John Gallo, my big brother and photo guru, who is dearly missed; Philip Ellison, my magic manuscript man, whose editorial expertise in the early days encouraged me to continue when I was lost for words; and my cheerleaders Denise Kachin, computer guru Valery Malin, Pat Mancuso, stylist Julie Opheim, Robert Skole, Janet Toney, Lee Weinstein, and Karen Goldade and my focus group.

My heartfelt gratitude goes to my original Beatle Buddies: Diane Brown, Joeanne Burns, Kathleen DeRosa, Betty Giello, and Andrea Gimbal. This story could not have come to life without them.

Grateful thanks go to Dr. Joe Palermo and Albert DiCaprio, who taught me early on about happiness.

There is a special place in my heart, and always will be, for Victor Spinetti, my muse and late friend. He believed in the book.

My very special thanks go to the dynamic Sam Lit and his late father, the Honorable Philly Deejay Hy Lit, "the man who brought the Beatles to Philadelphia." Thanks to Mark Lapidos, of the Fest for Beatles Fans, who graciously invited me to share the stage with Victor to discuss our fan club and the proposed book. My gratitude to the now-defunct *Philadelphia Evening Bulletin* and to the *Philadelphia Daily News* and *Southwest Globe Times* newspapers for a variety of outstanding articles on Beatlemania and pop culture. I give special thanks to the talented former *Philadelphia Evening Bulletin* photographer the late Sam Nocella; his playful photo of my memorabilia and me first appeared in 1974.

Big Beatle hugs to my daughters Jane and Margaretha, whose love and help encouraged me to carry on. Let me also thank all the readers of this book, young and old. I sincerely hope they enjoy their walk down my own Abbey Road to a time and place far removed from today.

Naturally, my sincere and humble thanks are extended to John, Paul, George, and Ringo. We love you. We always will. Thanks for the music and the merriment!

FOREWORD

Meet Patricia Gallo-Stenman, who fell in love in the early 1960s. But first, a short flashback.

Among the highlights of Ron Howard's collaboration with the White Horse Pictures film *The Beatles: Eight Days a Week* were the rip-roaring, eye-popping interviews with the fans from the early years. All are funny, sensitive, and passionate. Before the premiere in London, Ringo jokingly said to me, "What the f——, Larry. This book is more like the Larry Kane life story, also starring the Beatles. You're in it way too much, Larry." And I said, "I just remember more than you do." And that is true. Aside from the "boys," as we called them, and their "live" music, I mostly remember the screaming, tear-filled, gyrating young women, their faces bathed in sweat, their voices screaming out, all with the sense that one of those four Beatles was singing directly to them.

The fans are a major part of that movie, and when people see them on the screen, they are in disbelief at their fanaticism and passion. I have always felt that the Beatles were a rite of passage for many of the fans, whose story has really never been told in a first-person way.

That is, until now.

Memory can be strange. Time erases memories, unless you are a newsperson like me, who remembers everything by life-cycle events and dates of major news stories.

Patricia Gallo-Stenman has an intimate memory.

Her diary, emblematic of the wave of fandom, and representing millions of others, cements her role as a living "whisperer" of life, as a devotee of John, Paul, George, and Ringo.

Her work, based on her recollections, is not what nonfiction writers would call traditional, but for getting into the mind of a Beatles fan beginning in 1964, you can't beat it. It is that nontraditional approach that makes this book so special. After all, how hard is it to find a personal diary that exposes the chills and thrills that teenagers felt—the love, the devotion, and even the words of distaste for the girlfriends of the Beatles?

When I traveled with the Beatles to all stops on the U.S. and Canada 1964 and 1965 tours, I never, at least in the first weeks, realized what it would mean to the zillions of fans and, on a personal level, to my lifelong identification with the greatest band in history.

But all the details of the fans are confirmed by Patricia's diary. She represents those fans as a true believer and, without being salacious, brings the reader the private thoughts of a girl in love.

Patricia is no longer a girl. She matured into a young woman, attended Temple University (go, Owls!), worked as a journalist in Europe, and wrote for the *Philadelphia Evening and Sunday Bulletin*, may it rest in peace. She also resurrects the presence of Hy Lit, one of the great Top 40 deejays of that generation. Her material is first-class, and her collection as a scrapbooker makes the Web look, at times, clueless.

This is the real thing. The professional biographers may get just a little jealous, but with rare exceptions, few were in that state of mind in the early 1960s.

Patricia has brought the karma to life.

Besides, she's from Philadelphia. And to this writer, *that* is very special.

Larry Kane
Spring 2018

A BEATLEMANIAC'S JOURNEY

SEPTEMBER 2, 1964

Kathy and I, camped at the back entrance of Philadelphia Convention Hall, had been waiting forever for John, Paul, George, and Ringo. It was approaching late afternoon. We had arrived at 9:00 A.M. and hidden behind the building before the police assembled the white barricades meant to hold back the thousands of desperate fans sure to swarm around the hall ahead of the 8:00 P.M. concert. In front of the granite building, groups of wide-eyed girls streamed into the area—Beatle business as usual—dressed in casual summer shorts and proudly adorned with Beatle badges. Many of the hopeful fans carried homemade banners proclaiming this the "City of Beatle Love, Loyal to Beatles 4-Ever." As I stood squinting in the sunlight, a four-foot-tall sketch of Ringo's face jounced past me, held high by an artistic fan. . . .

As the hours dragged on, Kathy and I were parched, sweaty, and cramped from crouching behind a pillar. Did we dare give up our perch and miss seeing them, arriving stealthily or in a burst of bravado? Unfortunately, our bladders won out, and we melted back over the barricades to join the now twelve thousand fans and police crowding the sidewalks. The ivory marquee announced matter-of-factly, and inaccurately,

TONIGHT
THE BEATLE
HI LIT M.C.
S O L D   O U T

I had the presence of mind to snap a photo of Kathy in front of the marquee with my Instamatic, including some of our school friends all behind the barricades. Everyone was there. Who would miss the Beatles' first concert in Philly? . . .

Excited screams rose every time a car went by in front of the hall. Word then went out that the group would be smuggled in via truck. Every time a truck passed, the screams grew shrill. By late afternoon, still no Beatles. Sadly, we vacated our post to rush home, dress mod, grab our cherished tickets, and catch the trolley back to Convention Hall.

. . . Again outside Convention Hall, in my hand I held tightly to my light green ticket. Printed on its face: THE BEATLES E U 3 CENTER ORCHESTRA. The concert was wonderful, although I only saw five minutes of it. You see, masses of girls stood on their seats; nobody saw anything! It surely wasn't the Beatles' fault. The show they put on was great! If only I could have seen them or heard them better, it would have been perfect!

A FAN-TASTIC INSIDER'S LOOK AT BEATLEMANIA

As the preceding excerpt from my diary points out, Beatlemania was real to so many of us in the 1960s. Yes, the Liverpool group had talent and savvy management, but at the core of the Beatles' success were the legions of fans, dubbed "Beatlemaniacs," who worshiped at the Beatles altar. The worldwide Beatlemania seen in cities like my own Philadelphia was a fan phenomenon. It was through the fans' devotion and support that this rock group grew into superstars. The Beatles remained on top because their unique talents kept their millions of followers in their sway, buying their records, and flocking to the concerts.

Diary of a Beatlemaniac puzzles how fan loyalty brought the Beatles to megastardom. It began with one fan and one scream, multiplied by millions. Now Beatlemania lives in the pages of rock history.

This diary, which I kept faithfully in a tiny loose-leaf notebook for eleven years, starting at age thirteen, is a peek into the heart of an inner-city girl of her day. The adolescence-sugared entries are the essence of the story: a baby boomer coming of age against the backdrop of Beatlemania in the Swingin' Sixties, from Beatle Paul to puppy love, pesky parents, the prom, and, finally, high school graduation.

This is Patti, a naive, ambitious, gangly eighth grader, growing through a time of national trauma following the Kennedy assassination and blossoming in tune to the Age of Aquarius. Along this teenage highway were the frenzy of fan clubs, meet-the-Beatles schemes, and classic concerts. The mid-1960s was a fascinating era for the fans who allowed themselves to be taken up by the rush of Beatlemania. This book will strike a familiar chord with many women: how many, as teenage girls, scribbled in secret diaries after midnight? How many wished they had kept those tiny journals so they could read snippets of their coming-of-age selves? How many glued cherished photos into oversized scrapbooks?

WHY *THIS* DIARY?

The Beatles were the musical icons of my generation, but at the core of their success were the legions of fans whom the press had dubbed "Beatlemaniacs." Mainly teenage girls, we Beatlemaniacs were a breed apart wherever we lived in the world. We all helped to make it happen. The Beatles became megastars, and we were the force behind the Fab Four. Their diehard fans were there supporting the group as they skyrocketed to fame and fortune. We were with them all the way. We loved them unconditionally and believed in their music—we showed them just how much by our adoration. We were proud that the Beatles were the greatest pop group of the twentieth century.

Can you imagine: Beatles concerts without screaming girls? Movie theaters screening *A Hard Day's Night* (dir. Richard Lester, 1964) without hundreds of teens wiggling and waiting for tickets, and no crowds lining airport routes? It is almost impossible to imagine a respectful silence at a Beatles concert, a cultural happening with no screaming Beatlemaniacs. In a way, it is the mania, with the band and its music, that has defined the mystique—reserving for the Beatles an important place in cultural rock history. Beatlemaniacs paved the group's way to fame with a bangle of gold records. Fans waited in line for hours to buy concert and movie tickets with their parents' cold cash; Beatlemaniacs bought Beatles bobbleheads, wigs, magazines, sneakers, and posters; they sent petitions and attacked the Beatles' negative press with a vengeance; at schools, they banded with others like them in Beatle Buddy groups—and these were only the outward trappings of the Beatlemania phenomenon.

In diary format, part I of this memoir tracks the milestones in the Beatles' era that were synchronous with Patti and her Beatle Buddies' high school lives in Philadelphia, Pennsylvania, from 1963 to the tumultuous 1966 concert at Shea Stadium in New York. As the first book to explore Beatlemania from a bird's-eye view, using a wealth of material from my Beatles memorabilia collection and original snapshots, this diary tells of an innocent's romp through the magic of a special moment in the 1960s and offers an insider's look at Beatlemania. How did young Beatlemaniacs think? What exactly was in a Beatlemaniac's personal treasure chest? How did the Beatle Buddies plan their attack, hoping to meet the group at a Philadelphia hotel? What did fans wear, and why?

Part II of the book features never-before-published, original interviews with two experts who were in the trenches: the late Philadelphian pioneer deejay Hy Lit—an early champion of the Fab Four—and the late British actor Victor Spinetti. I interviewed Hy in 1964 and again forty-two years later. When Spinetti, the charming Welsh actor who costarred in the Beatles' films, appeared onstage at Philadelphia's Forrest Theatre in 1964 in *Oh What a Lovely War* (prod. Gerry Raffles and Joan Littlewood, 1963), I was there. At a time when ordinary kids could meet a celebrity and start a fan club, Spinetti found himself in the midst of the Beatlemania hype and then a part of the Philadelphia Beatle Buddies' lives. And so was born the Official Victor Spinetti Fan Club of America and a friendship that lasted nearly forty-eight years.

What, Exactly, *Is* a Beatlemaniac?

To avoid confusion, let's take a closer look at the differences between a Beatlemaniac and an ordinary fan—two very distinct species. True Beatlemaniacs lived, dreamed, and schemed to meet their favorite group, whereas typical fans merely enjoyed the Beatles' music and films. It was the difference between being a fanatic and being a fan. Beatlemaniacs were addicted to the thrill of all things Beatles.

Though countless books have focused on the Beatles' lives, loves, music, photographs, and relationships, it is left to the Beatlemaniacs to tell the rest of the story. These unsung fans are growing older, and without an effort to set the record straight, their tales will all too soon fall into fan folklore. If we are mentioned at all, we are often portrayed as fainting, hysterical, and "not all there." Fortunately, the story of what really happened to Beatlemaniacs can still be told.

And so this diary tells the familiar Beatles saga, but through the eyes and voice of an original teenage fan and her Beatle Buddies who lived the phenomenon of Beatlemania, in what we now call real time, in the blue-collar neighborhood of Southwest Philadelphia. The diary entries include my own vintage *Teen to Teen* newspaper columns, extensive scrapbook excerpts, news articles, original poetry, vintage ads, interviews with Beatle Buddies, letters from actor Victor Spinetti, fan magazines, and bits and pieces of nostalgia.

The Beatle Buddies were real, as were our experiences. This is not a work of fiction but rather a true story of a more innocent time when energetic teenage girls were excited by the music, the era, and the chase. Clearly our world has changed significantly over the past decades. Much of what the Beatle Buddies found exciting in the mid-twentieth century will today seem odd, out of date, and extremely naive. The average teenager today is light-years away from her 1964 counterpart. Keep this in mind when reading the diary: our group wholeheartedly believed in the Beatles, their music, and the pop culture. Throughout it all, we remained steadfast in our devotion—but this also meant adopting another lifestyle outside of the conservative boundaries of school and home. This was a brave move for those of us in the 1960s who attended strict, all-girls Catholic educational institutions and lived by the rigid rules of the day.

As a true Beatlemaniac who chronicled the world of a Beatles fanatic in real time, I reintroduce my experiences after more than a half-century and show how, in their own way, the Beatles helped me form my first true identity, taught me how to reach out to people, and sharpened my appetite for writing. I was introduced to the world of journalism when I was trying to wrangle a press pass from a local weekly newspaper to meet the Beatles in September 1964. The editor did not offer me a pass but suggested that if I would write about teenagers, the paper would consider printing some of my articles. Naturally, we were not paid. My friend Diane and I alternated columns, and I continued until my years at Temple University as a journalism student.

Indeed, I later went on to join the *Philadelphia Evening and Sunday Bulletin* as a staff writer, left five years later for grad school in Europe, married, and welcomed identical twin daughters. Most of my adult life has been centered in Finland, Texas, and Sweden, while following my career in writing.

But I still cherish those years when the Beatles were fab. Even now, when I hear the first strains of "I Saw Her Standing There," I am once again that gangly fifteen-year-old with braces on her teeth, stars in her eyes, and Paul on her mind.

Some things never change.

Dear John, Paul, George, Ringo: It Was a Very Hard Day's Night . . . but Let It Be

As far back as the 1970s, I believed the story of life as a Beatlemaniac should be told to the world. Following are an article and sidebar I wrote as a young staffer at Philadelphia's metropolitan daily paper and that appeared in *Discover, The Sunday Bulletin Magazine.* Not exactly nostalgia, the article was published on February 10, 1974, a scant four years after the group had disbanded, and it shows that even after the band's breakup, the Beatles lived on in the minds and hearts of their ardent followers.

Although this *Discover* article is a time capsule for the Beatlemaniac experience four years on, it is the diary that explores in real time the inner life of a self-confessed Beatlemaniac.

Here is how it all began.

Dear John, Paul, George, Ringo:

It was a very Hard Day's Night...

But Let It Be

By PATRICIA T. GALLO

My life changed on the night of Feb. 9, 1964 — the evening the Beatles made their first appearance on Ed Sullivan's tv show.

My friends and I knew about the Beatles, of course, and had heard their music. Now, we had a chance to see what the Liverpool quartet really looked like.

We fell in love with the Beatles that night and from then on, it was pandemonium.

Most of us selected our favorite Beatles that night. There was John Lennon, the married Beatle; Paul McCartney, the boyish one with dark hair; Ringo Starr, who wore outlandish rings, and George Harrison, dubbed the quiet one because he had a sore throat during that first American tour.

Diane adored John; Kathy cried over Ringo; Betty went into hysteria over Paul and Joanne learned to play the guitar like George.

They were members of my Beatle squadron at Philadelphia's West Catholic High School for Girls, where we were freshmen.

We were 14 — a naive, inbetween age. We were old enough to wear lipstick and kneesocks. Old enough to travel across town but too young to see certain movies. Old enough to scorn hopscotch but too young for dating.

At my all-girl parochial school, identical nuns drilled uniformed students in Latin, algebra and science. We students ran to classes wearing faceless bouffant hair styles.

We needed something else and we found it in the Beatles. The chase to see and meet our idols was on.

I first read about the Beatles in a Sunday magazine supplement during the 1963 Christmas season. I remember looking at the photo of hysterical girls at a concert and wondering just what generated such frenzy. After the holidays, pop radio station WIBG began to play two early Beatle hits,"I Want To Hold Your Hand" and "I Saw Her Standing There."

I got into the spirit and bought Capitol's "Meet The Beatles" album for my friend Kathy's birthday. On the record sleeve was a photo of the four heads partially silhouetted in gray tones. They looked like slightly impish choirboys.

In the early 60's the Beatle hair style was considered radically long — it covered their eyebrows but barely covered their ears. The four wore collarless suits, or velvet lapeled jackets at concerts. They promoted high-heeled boots for men. They were slim, young, and reminded me and my friends of the boys next door.

Not many singers then had the boyish spirit they possessed. At 14, I liked these characters who ate jellybeans, were baffled by their own success, and joked about their popularity.

At school, we began to talk about this new group whose music had a driving rock n' roll sound similar to American artist Chuck Berry. We enjoyed the simple beat; the earlier lyrics were easy to remember. "She loves you. Yeh, Yeh, Yeh."

There was a barrage of stories on the group in January, 1964, before their first American tour and that historic Feb. 9 debut. And another album, "Introducing the Beatles" on Vee-Jay records came out.

I and my Beatle squadron were hooked.

We would stop at nothing in our attempts to meet them and we would defend them to the death. A child psychiatrist said at the time that "They're just a fad. And the fad will fade . . .

ITEMIZED BEATLE SOUVENIRS
Owned by an Average Beatlemaniac

17 Beatle albums
2 Beatle buttons
2 "John Lennon" caps
1 Beatle scarf
1 ceramic Beatle charm bracelet
1 pair of Beatle decorated sneakers
4 8" Beatle dolls
1 box of Beatle stationery
101 Beatle bubblegum cards
19 Beatle fan magazines
3 paperback books
1 copy of John Lennon's book of poetry "In His Own Write."
1 "Cellar Full of Noise," by the late Beatle manager Brian Epstein.
1 6' life size poster of Paul MacCartney playing guitar
1 4' wall poster of The Beatles
2 Beatle scrapbooks of newspaper and magazine clippings.

10

It's all a perfectly normal part of growing up."

We didn't believe it. The Beatles were here for good, we thought, and child psychiatrists with silly theories were the ones who would fade away.

Our parents seemed to tolerate the Beatles. But then, they had no choice. Beatle music constantly blared from living room stereos.

I guess our parents thought the Beatles were nice safe boys who lived across the Atlantic somewhere and doubted that we'd ever get close enough to see them.

It's also true that some parents tolerated more than others.

Except for the floor, every inch of Diane's bedroom was covered with Beatle photographs. There was John smiling from the ceiling; Ringo in an old-time bathing suit; George riding in a go-cart; strips of Beatle wallpaper.

It was a shrine where many a Beatle fan paid homage. Looking back, I wonder how her mother ever cleaned the place or stood all those teenagers making a pilgrimage to the second floor.

Our parents also knew that part of our allowances went to buying Beatle junk. Our allowances varied but on the average we received about $5 a week. That covered school lunches, subway tokens and church collection envelopes. Whatever we could save out of that, plus the bonus money we managed to finagle from our parents, went to buy Beatle records, magazines, buttons.

Some adults, of course, took a dimmer view.

One teacher confiscated my entire Beatle bubblegum card collection during English class. She did have the good conscience to return it after nonchalantly shuffling through all the cards.

Beatle hair cuts began to bloom around school. It basically was a bowl cut with straight bangs which ended on the eyebrows. We pinned laminated Beatle buttons on our purses and coats. The most popular button styles said, "I Love the Beatles," and "I Love (Paul, George, John, or Ringo)." The latter button indicated undying dedication.

The true trademark of a Beatlemaniac was the "John Lennon" cap, a variation of the English school boy cap. They were sold in a variety of fabrics including velvets, plaids and denims. Every devoted Beatle fan owned one and wore it proudly both summer and winter.

We had our individual touches too. A Ringo fan wore many rings. A Paul fan learned to forge his signature on the inside covers of marble copybooks. I still make the "P" in my name like the "P" in Paul's signature. A sincere

Continued on page 12

follower of George owned a black leather jacket like the one he wore in early promotion photos.

My squadron saw the Beatles' first movie, "A Hard Day's Night," six times and memorized the script.

The movie, which premiered in 60 area theaters on Aug. 5, 1964, was directed by Richard Lester, a former Philadelphian. It focused on one zany day in the life of the group. For months thereafter we tried unsuccessfully to track down Lester's family in the Philadelphia phone book.

And then there was the first area concert.

Tickets for the Sept. 2, 1964 performance at Philadelphia's Convention Hall were sold almost as soon as they were put on sale. Fans camped for hours in front of the box office to purchase them.

On the morning of the concert, Kathy and I arrived early with a "plan." We cased Convention Hall and stationed ourselves in a lower level garage near the back entrance. We thought if we hid there before the police barricades went up, we might see the group when they arrived. After being holed up for five hours we emerged tired and hungry and saw the street flooded with teen-age girls. There were girls carrying color posters of Ringo, girls wearing Bermuda shorts and John Lennon caps, and girls from different factions of Beatle fan clubs saturating the area with membership pamphlets.

The police and their barricades lined the entrance of the hall — but still no Beatles. Every time a suspicious truck would pull up to the curb, some poor fan would start shrieking and start a chain reaction. We never saw the four arrive.

I didn't see or hear the Beatles that night. All I got were a few quick glimpses of Ringo's drum set, high on the stage. Everybody stood on chairs and screamed, cried and fainted. Many of the unbolted seats on the main floor tumbled over. Diane still proudly wears a leg scar where a chair plus one fan fell on her. The rest of the row fell on someone else.

After the show we felt that fate had dealt us a terrible blow. We had neither seen nor heard the group and had failed in our attempts to meet them.

Besides screaming our adoration, we wrote seething letters to critics who panned the group in the papers. Sometimes we even sent petitions. We had a running feud with Bulletin's critic Rex Polier, who once wrote "The Liverpool lunatics owe their sudden American TV popularity to the rating battle."

We also entered Beatle contests. I won $25 for my essay on "Why I Like The Beatles," and a teen-age fan magazine published my poetry. Diane became a finalist in a "Meet The Beatles in Atlantic City" contest, but didn't win.

We were one step closer to the quartet when we founded the Official Victor

Spinetti Fan Club of America, Chapter One in September 1964.

Spinetti, a Welsh actor, had appeared in "A Hard Day's Night," and was a close friend of the group. He was acting at the Forrest Theatre in "Oh What A Lovely War" and we camped outside the stage door during rehearsals until we met him.

After returning to London, Spinetti sent us the fuzzy gray sweater he wore in the first Beatle film. In August, 1966, while waiting in line to see the second Beatle movie "Help," we sold fuzzy samples of sweater lint. Diane, who was co-president of the club with me, wore the blanket-like sweater in the August heat.

Our sweater received the publicity it deserved after we made Bulletin columnist James Smart an honorary member of the fan club.

Spinetti proved both a friend and a contact. He also appeared in "Help," and the Beatles' "Magical Mystery Tour," and, while filming "Help" with the group on location, he sent us souvenirs. Diane was awarded a cigarette once smoked by John, Joanne received a blue candle off of George's 21st birthday cake, and I was given a cocktail stirrer used by Paul at a Nassau club.

We received all four Beatles' autographs on a plane menu called "The Beatles Bahamas Special." A birthday postcard arrived for me from Paul. It included my most treasured memento — a lock of Paul's hair from the hairdresser at Twickenham studios in London. The hair, which I encased in clear plastic, became a holy relic to all Beatlemaniacs who were allowed to view it.

The Beatle movement was not without its ripoffs. A sincere crook sold us "press conference" tickets at $5 each for the Beatles' Shea Stadium concert in New York city on Aug. 23, 1966. The only thing we got were blank stares at the press gate and from the police.

A magazine ad promised fans one inch squares of material, former pillow cases, where the Beatles had laid their shaggy heads. Another ad was selling pieces of rug from the group's hotel room. And scalpers had a field day with concert tickets.

For two and a half years we chased the Beatles.

We all learned Liverpool slang words such as "luv," "fave," and "gear." We devoured information published in fan magazines about George's collar size and frantic Beatle romances. I hosted birthday parties every June 18 for an ever-absent Paul. The long distance phone calls to Liverpool never quite made it. When both George and Ringo were married, we watched over the red-eyed members of our group.

It took us time to realize we weren't getting responses to our fan letters, and the scatterbrained meeting plans wouldn't work. And if we had met them, what then? We never made any long range post-capture plans. It was the chase to meet them which excited us.

We never made it.■

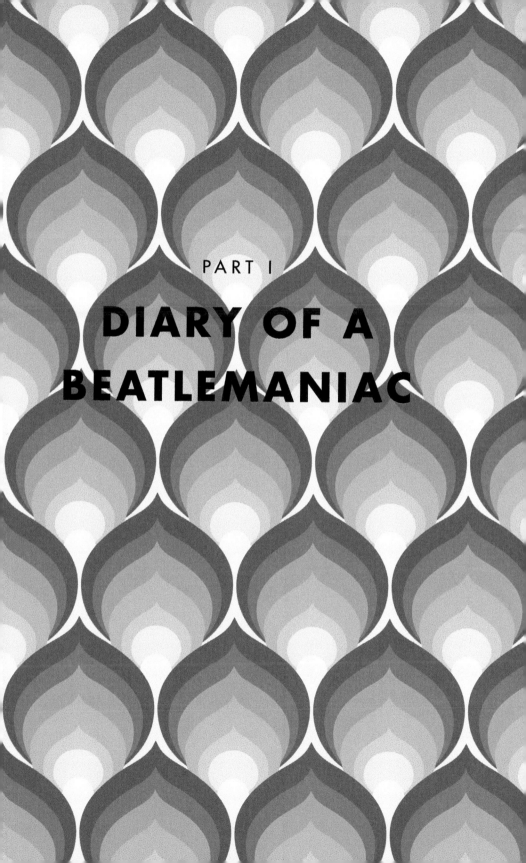

PART I

DIARY OF A BEATLEMANIAC

WINTER 1962–1963

DECEMBER 10, 1962

On this day of December 10, 1962, I, Patti Gallo, have finally found a use for you. I have owned you since last summer and could not find any uses for you. You were too small to draw in and too good to use for a homework assignment book. From this day on, anything that is interesting I will include in "My Little Black Book."

I'll tell you a little bit about myself. My heroines are Louisa May Alcott, Juliette Low, Mrs. Eleanor Roosevelt, Helen Keller, Mrs. Kennedy, Anne Frank, my mom, and Our Lady. I am thirteen and a half. I am not at all pretty and am very plain, with long, black hair and, of all things, a large nose. I'm not exactly Jackie Kennedy, but I am satisfied and would rather look plain than like the other girls my age with teased hair, makeup, and high-high heels.

I am different from most girls. I love to read, and people call me a bookworm. I also like school (sometimes) and get very good marks at

St. Clement's Grade School. I love animals, especially horses and dogs, more than anyone I know. Most girls my age are just the opposite of me. I don't know whether this is good or bad. I often think that I should have been born a hundred or maybe seventy years ago. For some reason, I am living in this era. I wish I knew why.

I live in Southwest Philly in one of the thousands of old brick row houses fronted by wooden porches. Many of the neighborhood dads do shift work at the nearby General Electric plant that looms over several blocks of Elmwood Avenue. On Muhlfeld Street, we are just about the only family with one child. Two Catholic families down the street each has an even dozen kids—in small three-bedroom houses. Cuban, Irish, Polish, Italian, and German are a few of the nationalities on Muhlfeld, so I get to sample some exotic food when I eat dinners at my friends' homes.

We used to live in South Philly when I was a little girl, just about ten minutes away over the Passyunk Avenue drawbridge. My folks, Jennie and John, were raised there, in the heart of the Italian section, where

there are even smaller row houses and narrower streets. Can you imagine? Dad left the neighborhood to fight with the 710 Tank Battalion in the South Pacific during World War II, while Mom helped assemble ships at the Philadelphia Naval Shipyard in South Philadelphia. They met on a blind date not long after Dad received his army discharge papers. I came along as a "49er" at St. Agnes Hospital only a couple of blocks down Broad Street from Dad's South Philadelphia High School. Mom is a homemaker; Dad works as a night manager for Linton's Restaurant. My grandparents were born in Italy and believe children should show respect at home. This means my folks are pretty strict with me. You know, listen to your elders, confession on Saturdays, church on Sundays, no talking back, dress modestly, get good grades . . .

To get away, I love to go to the movies on Friday nights at the Benn or Benson theater on Woodland Avenue with my friend Kathy, who is always falling in love with one of the skinny ushers. She puts her feet on the seat in front so that the guy comes by to flash his light on her. It never goes further than that, but at least she feels, in a strange way, that she gets noticed. My favorite movie star is Charlton Heston. Kathy and I went back to see *Ben Hur* four times, but she liked costar Stephen Boyd, and we didn't talk to one another for a while.

JANUARY 9, 1963

I haven't written here lately because I've been so busy. School has been in session for a week, but this morning, about five, I got sick. I'm OK now, only a little worried about exams. Not for long though, for they are next week. I can't help it, but I feel I am going to be a writer or something. I started this little diary because I read somewhere that girls used to keep diaries like this about a hundred years ago. So here goes.

JANUARY 21, 1963

Exams have been over since Friday. Today is Monday. I'm so glad, and I did very well . . .

FEBRUARY 6, 1963

I have been home with the mumps for three days now. I look like a chipmunk. Not a pretty sight.

FEBRUARY 23, 1963

I am back to school now and back to the same old grind. I love to read and wish our branch library had more books I wanted to read. Today, while at the main library in the city, I realized all the wealth and knowledge I am losing. I must make the best of our small library and not complain. At least I have books to read. In many places in this world, people don't even know how to read—and to think I am complaining about not enough books! Well, see you soon.

MARCH 15, 1963

Tomorrow I will go to the dentist. I wonder about the grand total of cavities. None or one or two I will settle for, but no more. A couple of years ago, I had six. My parents were not happy with the dentist's bill, and I promised to cut down on the sugary treats. I love chocolate in any shape, so this is hard for me.

Summer is around the corner. Rather, it's two months off. I like to exaggerate a bit.

MARCH 19, 1963

If someone gave me a million dollars, what would I do with it? I have often thought this out, and my answer has always been similar. First, I would hire a couple of maids to do all the housework for my mother. Then I'd buy the best string of horses you ever saw and a beautiful thoroughbred for myself. I would buy a big old-fashioned house in the country and lots of land to roam on. There would be a big stable for the horses and a bunch of grooms. Then I would be done my buying, except for an occasional sports car or two, and maybe a yacht. I would invest the rest of the money (if there was any left).

Gosh, I forgot the trips for Mother and Dad, as they always wanted to travel. But I'd stay home with the horses. Ah, such dreams I have . . .

MARCH 22, 1963
Tomorrow we take our high school placement test, but I am not that worried. You know something funny? I am not worried, for as the great Roosevelt put it, "The only thing we have to fear is fear itself."

SPRING–SUMMER 1963

APRIL 30, 1963

In two days, it will be my fourteenth birthday. I am going into my second year of being a teenager, and so far no boys have even looked at me. They go for the pretty ones who know what to say at the right time. Unfortunately, I am not pretty, nor do I know what to say at the right time. But I don't mind, for there is plenty of time for boys and plenty of time to go on dates. I am glad for Eileen, who is going with a boy named Eddie, but I do think fourteen is a little too young to go in a car with him or get a ring. Maybe I'm old-fashioned, but that's the way I feel. I also want to say that it's a lot of baloney when people say that "boys go for the old-fashioned girls." Ha Ha. If they do, they sure don't show it.

MAY 6, 1963

It's me again! Gee, I was just thinking about me. I can't do anything right. No, I am not kidding. Everything I do turns out backward or upside down. I am a bumbling idiot, and I am so disgusted of doing everything wrong that I just laugh it off. I find that it helps a lot when you do that. I just wish I could do something great so I can show people that I am not always a big dope who trips over her own feet. I wish I could save someone's life or win a prize for a poem. I would like to write a book that would be a big seller. Maybe I would be the most highly sought actress in Hollywood. I don't know why, but I'm always dreaming! (Giggle!)

JUNE 15, 1963

We are out for the summer now and all is well. I have been writing in you a half of a year already. We have been through a lot together, haven't we? I read in a magazine that if you are fourteen or fifteen and have never been out on a date, not to worry, for boys usually go for the popular girls, while some of the nice ones are left behind. So I'm not worrying that something is wrong with me anymore . . .

JULY 13, 1963

Oh, how I wish I could make something of myself. Ever since I was small, I've wanted to be somebody, not just anybody. To be looked up to and smiled upon. I know it's a long struggle up, as anyone knows . . . I often wish I were rich! Gee, to have a maid of my own or tell a chauffeur to take me a certain place and off I go! I sometimes picture how it would be, me as a daughter of society and a great equestrian. When I wake up, a maid changes my bed linens. After, I have a wonderful breakfast complete with maids and butlers. I wonder if I am the only one who has these types of dreams.

AUGUST 14, 1963

I'd like to write a little about walks. I always take a walk when I am puzzled about something. When you take a walk, the world seems brighter. All you need to do is look up to the blue sky with the white puffy clouds, and instantly, everything seems a little brighter. Your mind always seems clearer after you take a nice walk.

Gee, one person I wish I could meet is Prince Charles. He is the heir to the British throne and is only fifteen. I'm fourteen. Hmmmm. Imagine having a British heir just my age. That can sure spur a lot of romance stories for girls thirteen and fourteen and fifteen!

SEPTEMBER 9, 1963

I have been thinking more and more about Prince Charles. Just think, one day he'll probably be King! How utterly fascinating! Oh, he'll most likely marry some rich duchess or even a princess. Oh, it's "so hopeless," but I'll keep on thinking of him.

AUTUMN-WINTER 1963-1964

OCTOBER 12, 1963

. . . The summer is a thing of the past and fading into the pages of yesterday. I think of last summer as a "book summer," for I read about thirty-five books before it was over. But still, by the end of the summer, no romance had entered my simple life. I don't think it ever will, for I'm such a bashful girl. I can't even bear to look into a strange boy's face. I'm glad no one notices, though, for I would be embarrassed if Kathy or one of my girlfriends were to notice.

NOVEMBER 10, 1963

This fall I started my freshman year at West Philadelphia Catholic High School for Girls. I now catch the No. 36 trolley every school day to Center City Philadelphia. In the wet weather, there are so many smelly coats packed around me that I can't breathe. Our school, which is an old granite fortress, houses no fewer than seven hundred ninth graders this year. It

means you get to know the girls in your classes and homeroom, but not everyone. There is a variety of orders of nuns who teach us Latin, French, algebra, science, English, and religion. Right now, I can't keep them all straight. I must say, they do understand what we freshmen are going through. I take so many books home that my arms ache. We students all look alike in our drab green serge uniforms and beige cotton blouses with Peter Pan collars. With my sallow complexion, I always look sickly.

You must really behave around the nuns, even more so than in grade school. "Big John" is the prefect of discipline. She really is OK, but one bad move and you get a personal invitation to visit her office on the first floor. She is the tallest nun I ever saw, so I am always on my best behavior. You may ask what constitutes "disciplinary action" at West. Let's start with uniform infractions, as in your uniform is too short. Regulations state the uniform skirt must reach the floor when you kneel in front of your homeroom nun. "Hiking up" the uniform to make it appear shorter is not a good move either. There are many no-no's: wildly teased hair, sassing, chewing gum, being driven to school in a car, and—worst of all—not wearing a uniform. Poor Louise spilled chocolate milk over hers; it was sent to the cleaners. Since many of us only own one uniform with numerous blouse changes, she arrived the following day wearing a regular skirt and handed a note to her homeroom sister. No matter. Wham! She landed in detention for slopping chocolate milk on herself.

Otherwise, each day is about the same: go to school on the trolley, come home on the trolley, do tons of homework, rinse out my stockings, and maybe watch TV before bed.

NOVEMBER 22, 1963

Every heart in the United States, and probably in the world, was heavy today. Our beloved president, John Fitzgerald Kennedy, was assassinated. We were in school when Father announced over the PA system that the president had been shot and it was not known how bad the wound was. This announcement came over at seventh period, while I was at Latin class. We were pretty sad but hopeful for the best. Then, during eighth-period English, as we were all ready to read Greek mythology, Father announced, "Pray for the repose of Mr. Kennedy's soul." That was the end, for the eyes of every girl in the room began to tear. Handkerchiefs floated like snowflakes around the room, and Sister St. Bernadette's handkerchief came out soon after. No one I have seen all day has smiled, and all look stunned and very bewildered. Oh, it is so sad and painful to see Mrs. Kennedy's solemn face. How will she tell her children—whose birthdays are both next week—their daddy is dead? Johnson was sworn in as our new president two and a half hours after our beloved president passed out of this world. Oh, pray that this country will bear up under this great strain and that our new President Johnson will help keep us together.

NOVEMBER 28, 1963

Today is Thanksgiving and time to give thanks. Most people are sad though, and not many have the spirit. Our beloved president was laid to rest Monday at Arlington Cemetery. Oh, what a waste. We all loved and admired him from the youngest to the oldest. This will most likely go down in history as another important fact to be memorized, but Kennedy as a man was a generous husband and father. His widow is holding up marvelously, not crying in public once. He was truly a legend in his own time, so maybe we do have something to be thankful for. We can also thank God that this country had someone to take over after Kennedy and that no riots took place to see who would get into office.

DECEMBER 10, 1963

Happy birthday! One year ago today I started writing in you. So much has happened: a new president, a new pope, a new school, a new feeling in people of grief but hope for the future. I am the same old me, though, for one year, or even one hundred years, can't change me. I still love animals, and I also still admire Mrs. Kennedy—even more so, for now we know what a valiant woman she is. Well, can't spend much time writing today, for it is Tuesday and I have piles of homework. I just wanted to say happy birthday to us and our lasting friendship.

JANUARY 1, 1964

Happy New Year to me! I spent part of the holiday time with my friend Andrea, who moved away from the neighborhood to the suburbs. Her dad just finished college and is now an engineer. I miss her a lot. We have been good friends for years and years. Always fun to stay in Springfield, see trees outside your bedroom window and use a dishwasher to clean up the family meals. The downside is that her younger sister and brother drive you crazy. Times like this make me appreciate being an only child. But I would like to be that only child with a tree outside my window and a dishwasher.

On Sunday, we read in the newspaper magazine about a new music group that is really popular in England. Pictures of screaming girls appeared with the black-and-white photos of the long-haired musicians. Why were the girls so nutty? I mean, it wasn't Elvis. I can't remember the name of the group.

JANUARY 20, 1964

Tomorrow is the last day of exams. I haven't been doing as well as I should, and I'm very worried. Oh, if everything were cheery again. I wish I were happy, but how can someone be happy when her school marks just slipped all the way down?

JANUARY 25, 1964

I feel much better than the last time I wrote in you. Just like last year, I have spring fever. Only this year I have learned not to get all choked up about it.

The truth is that I have grown up! No more silly, hopeless dreams for me.

I'm going after reality. I just hope I can stick to this policy. Learning to do the right thing, such as believing in reality, is hard sometimes. I must learn to grow up and stop believing in those crazy fairy tales!

FEBRUARY 3, 1964

Ah, a year ago today I got the mumps. I should be so lucky to come down with something this February. We have religious retreat this week. Exams have been over for a while, but I wish it were summer.

FEBRUARY 7, 1964

Today is my best buddy Kathy's fifteenth birthday. What do you buy for someone who has the complete collection of Berenstain Bears books? I was shopping at the A&P supermarket with my mom and happened to spot the revolving LP record display rack with new releases. There was an album featuring the same group from England that was featured in the newspaper during my visit to Andrea. The album is called *Meet the Beatles*. On the record sleeve is a super photo of four heads partially silhouetted in gray tones. They look like slightly impish choirboys. I figured this would make a great birthday gift for Kathy. I paid $1.99 at the A&P and didn't go over my birthday budget.

When I got home and looked through the daily paper, I saw where Lit Brothers department store is also selling *Meet the Beatles* (monaural) for $1.99. In stereo, the price is $2.49. These are "Lit's low prices—3 days only."

FEBRUARY 9, 1964

My life changed for real tonight. The Beatles were on *The Ed Sullivan Show*! I almost died. Paul looked just like he did on the record sleeve, only cuter. He is a real ham in front of the camera. I can't believe the first time I saw them was just after Christmas. They have grown so popular in such a short time. I remember that the first magazine photos were a bit blurry and dark, but I knew right then I liked Paul. Radio station WIBG now plays two Beatles songs, "I Want to Hold Your Hand" and "I Saw Her Standing There."

Then I got into the spirit when I bought Capitol's *Meet the Beatles* album for Kathy. She loved it!

This is what I know so far about them. There are four Beatles: John Lennon, the married Beatle; Paul McCartney, the boyish dark-haired one; Ringo Starr, who wears oodles of rings; and George Harrison, whom they call the quiet Beatle. (Poor baby has a sore throat, I heard.)

When Ed Sullivan introduced them on coast-to-coast TV tonight, those lucky girls in the audience started to scream. I wonder who they knew to get those coveted tickets in New York! The Beatles sang five songs: "All My Loving," "Till There Was You," "She Loves You," "I Saw Her Standing There," and "I Want to Hold Your Hand." I didn't want it to end.

Why the Beatles? Why are we so excited over them? In my own case, I guess, it is because they are so different. They come from far away with a different yet familiar look and sound. The music is familiar, yet it isn't. The accents are unusual to me, but the words are in English. They are rough yet smooth. Enchanting but dangerous. OK, I also need *something* good to listen to and look at right now. I'm fourteen. I'm old enough to travel across town but too young to date. I can wear lipstick but not see certain movies. I get drilled at school in "exciting" subjects—Latin, algebra, and science. I need *something* to keep me from utter boredom.

FEBRUARY 11, 1964

It snowed very hard today, Tuesday, and we had off from school. Tomorrow we have to go back though. Oh, nuts. The Beatles have really hit the United States by storm. We all love them over here and wish they could stay longer, for they are leaving next week. They sing swell, but our homeroom nun thinks they are "too forward" and a lot of other things that are not nice. Our religion nun said she thought they looked like they needed a bath, which was not nice either. They are *the* singing group from England, and even New York columnist Dorothy Kilgallen and Ed Sullivan really like them, so they can't be that bad! I think they're rather cute.

Paul is still my favorite.

FEBRUARY 15, 1964

I had a wonderful dream about Paul last night. It was in color and so real. It was even in two parts. Oh, I like to think that it was real and that now I'm dreaming. But all good things must come to an end, and that dream sure went fast.

As I said—all good things must come to an end, so "Bye for Now."

FEBRUARY 16, 1964

Once again, it was Ed Sullivan with the Beatles. Kathy and I watched the show, which was aired live from Miami Beach. Tonight they sang "She Loves You," "This Boy," "All My Loving," "I Saw Her Standing There," "From Me to You," and "I Want to Hold Your Hand."

We could not believe how great they look on TV. Ed Sullivan really knows how to pick talented guest artists. My mom watched the show, too, but I don't think she knew what to make of them. She has always been a Frank Sinatra fan. She did say that the girls called "bobby-soxers" used to swoon over Sinatra at live performances. History does repeat itself.

FEBRUARY 24, 1964

Bought a second Beatles album. This one is *Introducing the Beatles* on Vee-Jay Records. The color album cover is not the best—it looks like it was taken a while ago, and the guys appear pale and rumpled in frumpy brown suits. But the songs are great. I especially like "Ask Me Why" and "A Taste of Honey" because they are so pretty and the harmonies work well.

MARCH 1, 1964

Well, Robert J. Williams now knows *not* to mess with Beatles fans. Hoards of us wrote in to the newspaper telling Mr. Williams what a jerk he was to come down so hard on the Beatles after watching them on *Ed Sullivan,* saying they are "as freakish as a two-headed lady." Wow, can you imagine the nerve of Robert J. Williams?

MARCH 3, 1964

A whole slew of journalists are getting in trouble after writing negative stuff about our boys. Now, Washington, D.C., columnist Art Buchwald has gotten into the thick of it.

Oh, no, et tu Buchwald? Kate, Guy, and Nelson belong to yesterday. We are now hip with John, Paul, George, and Ringo.

MARCH 10, 1964

They are calling it "Beatlemania," and now it is taking West Catholic by storm, except the nuns are on the warpath. During the past couple of weeks, here is what has happened. Beverly has been selling Beatle buttons (the black-and-white variety) in art class. So far she hasn't gotten caught by Sister. We freshmen were lectured by our Irish homeroom nun following *The Ed Sullivan Show* on those "dirty unwashed Englishmen with no talent on TV." I believe she thinks they have a one-way ticket to hell and that they are condemning our

The Beatles' Defenders
By ART BUCHWALD

Buchwald

Washington—It shall follow as the day the night that anyone who writes about the Beatles will receive hundreds of letters from teenagers protesting the defamation of their idols. Ever since we suggested that the only way to stamp out the Beatles was for parents to say they liked them, the mailman has been dumping envelopes on our desk filled with threats, pleas and denunciations.

We have been called, not necessarily in alphabetical order, a fink, a stuffed shirt, an old fogey, a rat, and worst of all, "an adult."

One young lady wrote, "It is with great difficulty that I am writing this letter to you as I do not want to lose my temper (and mine is very violent) but you had no right to attack the Beatles. I would like to ask you how you can defend the goldfish - swallowing, zoot suits, and flagpole-sitting of your generation, and attack us for liking the Beatles."

"How can you attack us," another teenager wrote, "when in your day you were crazy about Vaughn Monroe? I'll bet your parents thought you were 'way out' too."

Three young ladies all chipped in for the same stamp to inform us they were sick and tired of everyone's picking on the Beatles and it was terrible to treat foreigners this way.

Another letter-writer felt that we didn't like the Beatles because of their hair. "It's silly to dislike someone because of the length of their hair. How would you feel if people stopped liking you because you were bald? Yeah, yeah, yeah!"

Still one more letter, unsigned, asked, "Why won't adults allow teenagers to enjoy life? We don't make fun of what our parents like."

From Bethesda, Maryland, comes word, "Boy, are you crazy! Why can't adults realize that the Beatles are the greatest experience one can go through? When I hear them my heart starts to pound and tears fill my eyes. I love the Beatles because they're sexy without trying to be and can sing. Yeah, yeah, yeah!"

In almost every case the letters demanded, "Why can't you like the Beatles?"

Since we can't answer all the mail, perhaps we'll do it in this column. The reason we don't like the Beatles is that we happen to be a fan of Guy Lombardo, Kate Smith and Nelson Eddy. If it hadn't been for the Beatles, perhaps Ed Sullivan would have booked them on his show for the past three weeks instead of the Beatles.

When Kate Smith sings "God Bless America," we go out of our mind. When Guy Lombardo sings "Dardanella," our heart starts to pound, and we don't think anything moves us as much as Nelson Eddy's singing "Shortnin' Bread."

When the Beatles came along, we must admit we became fiercely jealous. Everyone forgot about Kate Smith, Guy Lombardo and Nelson Eddy, and all they could talk about was John, Paul, George and Ringo. Every time we called a disc jockey and asked him for "When the Moon Comes Over the Mountain" or "Rose Marie," he hung up on us. If you were a grown-up, wouldn't you be bitter, too?

Now it's out in the open. We were trying to sabotage the Beatles so our favorites would be up there again.

young immortal souls to damnation. I stuck a homemade Beatles calendar inside my locker door to cheer me up in the mornings. The nun on locker room duty snatched it off my door before I could explain.

At least I wasn't sent to after-school detention. That will be reserved for Beverly when she gets caught selling buttons. I almost went to detention today when Sister St. Bernadette confiscated my new deck of Beatles bubblegum cards. She caught me showing the cards before class, marched down the aisle, and took them back to her desk. After shuffling through them, she made a face, and I was sure they were going to be thrown in the trash. She waited until after eighth period and kindly returned them with a dire warning. That was sheer luck, and so she remains my favorite teacher.

You can't imagine it, but Beatle haircuts are popping up at school. Mainly short bobs with long, straight bangs, they are not that flattering teamed with drab uniforms. Some of us pass Beatles magazines in class and hope we don't get caught. Funny thing is, we Beatles fans are starting to band together. I imagine there is safety in numbers.

Kathy and I took a walk in the park on Sunday afternoon proudly wearing our Beatle buttons on our winter coats while clutching our favorite magazines. We posed in front of the dentist's office, where we snapped a few pictures. Long live the Beatles!

MARCH 20, 1964

Listening to Beatles music got Kathy in trouble at home. Honestly. Kathy, who is also known as "Spindles," because she is skinny, broke the sink in the family's only bathroom. Before school, she was listening to the Beatles' new single "Can't Buy Me Love" on the radio while brushing her teeth. She was really getting into the beat, using the sink as a drum set, when the top fell off the pedestal. Oops! Not a good day for Spindles. Kathy adores Ringo, so it was only natural she got carried away with the music.

Kathy has light, straight, shoulder-length hair and side bangs she is always combing. She adores classic movies and styled her hair just like actress Dorothy Lamour. Now she is growing out Beatle bangs. For a joke, I bought her an enormous plastic comb. She didn't think it was too funny. We went to grade school together, and she lives only a couple of blocks from our house near Devine's Tap Room. Her dad works the day shift at General Electric on Elmwood Avenue, and her mom hails from a big Irish family.

SPRING–SUMMER 1964

APRIL 2, 1964

Recently I made new friends at school who absolutely adore the Beatles. Here we are—the Beatle Buddies. We are rough and tough and ready to meet our idols—under any circumstances. The Beatles brought us together. Actually, we are the rejects who don't fit the "prom queen" and student council image—except for Jean.

Our inner circle:

There is Jean, who looked twenty-one when she was born. Jean is a George fan. She lives and breathes George. She is taking music lessons in town to play guitar—like George. Jean is tall and well built, with sleek, straight brown hair, a smudge of freckles, and a winning way. She is the only one of our group to date. We feel it is a bit disloyal to the cause, but nevertheless. It is Jean who has fantasies about George and their imaginary twins. She comes home from school with us on the El, and as we climb the steps to the train platform, she tells us what George and the twins did the day before. Suddenly we forget the algebra test and the smelly gym suits we are carrying. We nod in agreement. Every one of us has the same thoughts about "her own" Beatle.

Diane is our Beatle leader. She is dedicated to John and was the first one of us to get a Beatle haircut. Diane is brown haired and fun loving. We absolutely love her and her room. Except for the floor, every inch of Diane's bedroom is covered with Beatle photographs. There is John smiling from the ceiling, Ringo in an old-time bathing suit, George riding in a go-cart, strips of Beatles wallpaper. Making a pilgrimage to the second floor is unlike anything else. It goes way beyond a sacred place. This is the holy of holies. This is Diane's shrine to the Fab Four.

Diane is one of the fans who does not hold a grudge against Cynthia. She is John's wife. Diane dotes over John's small son Julian. She thinks there is enough of John to go around to all his fans. She is more tolerant than most fans, who want to scratch the eyes out of the Beatle wives and girlfriends. Diane is pretty classy.

Barbara with her cat-eye glasses and soft brown hair looks like she is quiet and studious, but don't let that fool you! She is in my homeroom and has a wicked sense of humor. Barbara is the dreamer among us and is deeply in love with Paul. She is really our rock, as she is so dependable. Barbara has piles of common sense.

ME (Patti): Fave Beatle is Paul. Nickname for Paul is "Jamie," since James is his first name. I am skinny with dark-framed glasses, braces, acne, and long, frizzy black hair. I am painfully shy and not a candidate to win the Miss America pageant in Atlantic City. Jane Asher-Smasher, who is Paul's actress girlfriend, is not one of my favorite people.

Kathy Spindles: Here is where the groups tend to overlap, since Kathy and I make up one tight little group, while Diane, Jean, Barbara, and I are in yet another one. In addition, there are those who are lone Beatlemaniacs and bounce around between groups. Among them:

Margaret, who is one of fourteen kids, goes to school with us. Ringo is her boy. She is always seen (except in class) wearing a dark-colored Lennon cap over her stringy blonde hair. Margaret has started to sign her name with a "star" for Ringo, and she is never without her oversized "I Love Ringo" button on her multicolored wool winter coat. Naturally, we are not permitted to wear any Beatle stuff on our school uniforms or we stand a good chance of landing in after-school detention.

Grace is our oldest Beatle Buddy, as she is nineteen, is out of high school, and works in an office. She lives in the neighborhood, and her dad has been with the railroad for years. Grace, who is big boned, has it bad for Ringo. She totes an oversized handbag that contains a large framed photo of the drummer. Grace's trademark is the many colorful rings she displays on her fingers, just like Ringo. She also clasps a St. Christopher medal around her neck, just like the one Ringo wears.

A true Beatles fan takes on the personality and traits of her favorite member of the group. Diane wears a cap like John, Grace loves lots of rings just like Ringo—and Jean is diligently learning to play the guitar like George. It makes us feel closer to *them.* So far, I have not met a Beatles fan who does not have a favorite, and not one of them claims more than one. So, one Beatle per fan is the norm. To be our very own. Sometimes I feel angry that so many girls have chosen Paul "the Cute One" as their fave. It isn't fair. Who is the most popular? Hard to say, but it could be John or Paul. One thing is for sure: Beatles fans are mighty possessive of the ones closest to their hearts. Look out if you say a bad word about John, Paul, George, or Ringo.

APRIL 19, 1964

Spring has been on its way, but it has been awful rainy. Spring is the season of *amour,* and it better start happening. The Beatles are still in the top 10, and Paul McCartney is still the cutest Beatle. Ah, when they come back to the United States, Kathy and I will be in the front row! (I hope.) School is a drag, and I can't wait for summer. It is so grueling to go to that school five days a week and get up so darn early. Oh, summer, hurry!

Now I got my copy of *The Beatles' Second Album* from Jolly's Record Store on Woodland Avenue. So glad they weren't sold out. Listen to it over and over on my stereo in the living room. My parents are not thrilled, as the family television is in the same room. I really like "You Really Got a Hold on Me," "Thank You Girl," and "You Can't Do That." Kathy likes "Money."

MAY 2, 1964

Happy fifteenth birthday to me . . . I just got back and am so tired. The Rosary Club from West Catholic went to New York to see the World's Fair. I really don't belong to the Rosary Club, but there were empty seats on the bus and I decided to go along with the group. Tried my hand at making rosaries on the drive up but became nauseated and nearly car sick. I wore my new gray mod dress with the white Chelsea collar. We had to wear our church clothes and dress shoes or the nuns would not let us near the bus. Enjoyed seeing Disney's "It's a Small World" pavilion. Kathy snapped a picture of me in back of Ringo's director's chair. Hope the picture doesn't turn out blurry, as she is not that great with a camera.

MAY 5, 1964

I am soooo very lucky. The tickets for the September 2 Convention Hall Beatles concert went on sale yesterday afternoon. I am sure glad I wasn't one of the 2,500 fans gathered outside the building. Kathy and I bought our tickets from Nick Petrella, who owns a popular record store in South Philly. Nick is close friends with my Uncle Dom and cousin Phil. Actually seeing, smelling, and squeezing that light green ticket makes me feel closer to the Beatles than I ever thought possible.

According to Rex Polier of the *Philadelphia Evening and Sunday Bulletin,* many kids had to cut school to get their tickets, and some even slept Sunday night on the steps at Convention Hall with blankets wrapped around them for warmth. Even though the police and Convention Hall staff chased the school-skippers away, they snuck back!

MAY 17, 1964

We have our own Beatles slang, which includes British words that the Beatles use and that are popular in London. You can tell you are among friends when you start throwing around the following:

```
A Cuppa = A Cup of Tea or Coffee
Birds & Dollies = Girls
Bloke = A Buddy or Friend
Cheeky = Flippant
Cheers = Good-bye, Thank You
Daft = Stupid
Fab = Great, Fantastic
Fave = Favorite
Groovy = Nice, Cool, Neat
Gear = Cool, Groovy, Fabulous
Luv = Love, or nickname for a friend
Jolly = Very Good
Mate = Friend
```

Smashing = Terrific
Ta = Thanks
Tah-Tah = Bye-Bye
The "Lads" = The Beatles
Thick = Stupid

MAY 25, 1964

The time is right to buy Beatles stuff. Woolworth's on Elmwood Avenue is selling Beatles dolls, Beatles bobblehead mascots ($2.22), Beatles wallpaper at 23 cents per yard, and even jewelry. I bought four Remco Beatles dolls, which are so cute. They have guitars, a tiny drum for Ringo, and rooted hair and cost me $3.77. If I had wanted to buy only Paul, I would have paid 99 cents. They came in great boxes with all four Beatles' pictures. I found the perfect spot to put them—on top of my stereo in the living room.

JUNE 5, 1964

"John Lennon" caps are now big with us fans. These were called schoolboy or seaman caps and were worn around Liverpool for years and years. John is especially fond of wearing caps. Right now, you can find them in a variety of colors and fabrics—everything from basic black wool to black velvet and even denim! They keep your head warm in winter, but boy, can you sweat in the Philly sun come this time of year. I wear my black velvet "John Lennon" cap proudly, but I am about to retire it for the summer. One of the ways Beatles fans identify one another is by their "John Lennon" caps.

JUNE 18, 1964

What happens when the Beatles can't be here for their birthdays? Host a birthday party—without the guest of honor. I was not sure where our Paul was on this particular day, but I hosted a party for him earlier today in my mom's dining room. No catered feast or air conditioning, only my Beatle Buddies and a cake from Wagner's Bakery on Elmwood Avenue. Written on top of the delicious white cream icing in fancy blue script was "Happy Birthday Paul." As a final touch, I plopped my Remco Paul doll on the cake, making his tiny boots sugary. Something was still missing. I designed a party hat for plastic Paul. The room needed a new look for such a festive occasion. I got creative and tacked some great color posters of our boys on my mom's new wallpaper and then borrowed her best polka dot glasses. No Paul? No worry. My guests and I snapped away with my Instamatic camera huddling around a lifelike photo of our missing McCartney. I also served butterscotch cakes, chocolate chip cookies, and pretzels. Too bad Paul missed the fun and the fab food.

Since our honored guest was not present, I decided to call him personally in Liverpool to send birthday wishes. My Beatle Buddies shook their heads in disbelief as I reached for the family telephone. I carefully dialed the overseas operator and placed a person-to-person call to the number I found in a fan magazine. The operator, who must have heard this type of thing a thousand times, chirped, "He's not in. Try his fan club, luv."

That made the whole party—actually *talking* to Liverpool and not paying for the call. Mom would have killed me.

JUNE 25, 1964

Things have changed. Why, yes, it is summer, but everything else spells misery. My long hair is cut now—my spirit broken. My faith in life is shattered. The only thing holding me together is love of the Beatles. If it weren't for that, I would have gone nutty long ago. My mother nags because I am not popular. How could someone possibly be popular with glasses, braces, and pimples together? One may be OK, but all three?

I think of Paul McCartney more and more here lately, but it does no good. I only love him more each day, while the chances of him loving me grow slimmer each dawning day.

Again, now that my hair is cut, it seems like I'm waiting for that old friend to return. I hope it grows by the Beatles concert in September! All the girls around the Beatles have long hair.

JULY 2, 1964

My feelings are still bitter. I am the exact opposite of what I want to be. I wish I looked like Jane Asher (Paul's girlfriend) with long, red hair, a tall girl with fair skin without a blemish on it. Instead, I have frizzy, dark, short black hair, olive skin, pimples, braces on my teeth, and bright white glasses with rhinestones. Paul McCartney would never go for me.

I am so very plain. Oh, how I would like to lock myself in some dark closet and never come out. The truth is that I am desperately in love with Paul, and I am so pimply and frizzy I could never hope to catch him.

THE BEATLE POEMS OF PATRICIA T. J. GALLO: NEARLY COMPLETE WORKS

THE HEAVY HEART
My tortured heart is sad,
For I'm in love with a lad.
Who could never love me?
So it's very sad you see.
But I'll always hope and pray,
That maybe there'll be a day.
My heart will be free,
Of loving Paul McCartney.

41

PAUL

By morning in the brightest light,
In evening at the greatest height.
I think of Paul with all might.
I can't help loving precious Paul,
So dark, quite handsome, and tall.
To me he will always be my all!!

SWEETNESS AND YOUTH

Young Love has passed me by,
As I waited with stars in my eyes.
For that boy so sweet that when he sang,
Every bell in my small heart rang.
Alas! Sweetness has gone forever,
The bells are returning never.
For very far across the sea,
He's with a starry lass like me.

"SONG OF PAUL"

How do I love thee,
Let me count the many ways.
Is it how you sing,
Or maybe the way you sway.
May it be your eyes of brown,
Or that lovely way you frown.
Might it be how you wear your hair,
Is that what brings me to tears?
Ah, it might be your voice so silky smooth,
Or your hands over the chords as they move.
Could it be your totally innocent face,
Or the ways you spread joy every place.
Can it be that manner so very sweet,

```
That seems to knock me off my feet.
Is this why I love thee,
Or is it not at all.
Could it be I love you,
Cause you're just Paul?
```

I am thinking of sending my poetry to some teenage magazines. Perhaps I can get published. These magazines are now printing poetry from fans of the Beatles. Hope my poems have a chance and make it into their pages. How exciting!

JULY 7, 1964

It is getting worse each day. It seems as if Paul has me under his spell and I can't escape. It's no good for me and ruining me to pieces. I saw a picture of Jane Asher, his girlfriend. The one I saw was a recent one. Now I find out that long-haired girls are Paul's favorites. I've always known it, but this picture proved it. For the Beatles concert, everyone is letting her hair grow long, but I am afraid mine is not growing fast enough.

Oh, Jane Asher and Paul keep on running through my head. I'm very jealous, I confess. Whatever happened to the old days when I was happy? These Beatles are sending me wonderfully nutty, but I wish Paul and Jane would break up.

Oh, happy birthday, Ringo!

JULY 15, 1964

Muggy summer's day with nothing much to do. My parents never take a summer vacation. Dad is always working. My last vacation was in August 1961, when Grandmom Gallo took me to Montreal and Quebec, Canada, to visit cathedrals. My knees still ache when I think of all that kneeling.

Earlier today I went to hang out with Diane. We spent the afternoon leafing through Beatles magazines in her room and listening to the music.

I browsed through a magazine to discover Paul's shoe and collar sizes—
and saw cute pictures of Cynthia and baby Julian.

JULY 29, 1964

Hi! I am still waiting for my hair to grow. I have decided that I must give
up Paul if I want to live like a human again. He is Jane's and to Jane he
goes. Let him.

I have found something to do, as I have been candy striping a lot here
lately and have put in forty-five hours of service as of today. I like it and
want to continue.

I am still the same me. Never-changing Patti. Mom says that people
think me quiet—perhaps because I love the Beatles so much. But didn't
they think Albert Einstein was a bit quiet and backward too? Poof at the
world. I'm an individual and very proud of it! Till again.

AUGUST 3, 1964

We all rushed to buy our copies of *Something New.* Jolly's Record Store
must be making a killing on all the Beatles albums they are selling to
us fans. I am a sucker for the ballads, especially those sung by Paul. Of
course, "And I Love Her," "If I Fell," and "Things We Said Today" are my
faves. "Any Time at All" has got a driving beat and is a bit unusual. Some
of the same songs appear on the new *A Hard Day's Night* album, too, but
that is OK. Who cares? I can listen to these songs over and over on my
stereo in our living room. I know I often complain about this, but I wish
the stereo was somewhere else. My folks always watch TV in the evenings,
so that cuts down on my listening time a lot. I hope my stereo will be in
my own room one day, but right now it is shared spaces for our family.

AUGUST 6, 1964

Yesterday was "B" Day. The Beatles' *A Hard Day's Night* movie premiered
in sixty theaters in the area. The film focuses on one zany day in the life
of the group. We had to get up early and take the bus to Upper Darby to

line up in the heat at the 69th Street Theatre, along with hundreds of fans. It was worth it! I loved seeing Paul in black and white running all over London. Some girls constantly squealed both before and during the film, while others vowed to return to see it over and over and over.

I read that some 1,600 fans lined up from early in the morning until the doors opened at 11:50 A.M. The movie started at 1:30 P.M., and the concession stand sold great Beatles stuff in the lobby—including Beatles portraits for a dollar. Before the movie started, we all began to chant, "We want the Beatles!" That's when they showed a movie trailer featuring singer Tom Jones.

At least we can go home after seeing A Hard Day's Night and listen to the sound track of the movie. I love the cover of the album, with its red, black, and gray bold colors—and all eight eyes peering out from under their "moptops." My favorite of all favorite cuts from the album is "And I Love Her"—so dreamy and wonderful. Paul sounds absolutely wonderful, as usual.

Kathy, Carol, and Maureen went to see the movie, too, but were escorted out of the theater for throwing black jelly beans at the screen. I hope their parents don't find out. I know they won't tell them, and I sure am not going to open my mouth to my folks. I imagine they just got carried away in the moment.

Everyone knows this Beatles movie was directed by former Philadelphian Richard Lester. As soon as we got home, Diane and I started searching for the Lester family in the local Yellow Pages phone book. Unfortunately, no one who answered knew who we were talking about. Of course, they could have lied. We won't give up! If Richard Lester has relatives within a fifty-mile radius of Philly, we will track them down sooner or later.

By the way, tickets to the movie, which opened in so many area theaters, went on sale last week at several places. At the Merben and Mayfair theaters on Frankford Avenue, more than one thousand fans had lined up in the hot sun by 11:00 A.M. Some girls had arrived as early as 6:30 A.M.

for their tickets. They opened the box office early and sold the fifty-cent under-twelve tickets and one-dollar adult tickets. The cute tickets had a picture of the Beatles on the front. When we bought tickets, they gave us round paper buttons that posed the question, "I'VE GOT MY BEATLES MOVIE TICKETS. HAVE YOU?"

AUGUST 16, 1964

I won a contest! I can't believe it! I entered the "Why I Love/Hate the Beatles" essay contest (one hundred words or fewer) in the *Philadelphia Daily News*—and won twenty-five dollars. The newspaper publishes positive and negative letters from the public. The nine judges include popular radio personalities such as Hy Lit from WIBG.

Every day the judges choose two winners and publish their essays. Mine was selected today. I was picked as a winner from the hundreds of entries. This is quite an honor, and the twenty-five-dollar prize is not bad either.

Their letter to me—

Dear Pat:
Congratulations on winning a prize in the Philadelphia Daily News "Beatles" letter-writing competition.

We are happy to enclose our check for $25 in payment of your award.

Again, congratulations from the *Philadelphia Daily News*.

Below is the actual winning letter that appeared in the newspaper on August 25. I am keeping a copy of the check in my Beatles Scrapbook!

> Here are two more winners among the Beatle letters and the runners-up. The two winners will be award $25 each. Meanwhile, the judges still have a lot of judging to do. A page of letters will appear in the *Philadelphia Daily News* each day. So keep sending those letters to the Beatle editor.

And this, my friends, is the essay:

It Pays to Say So
They came to us in the midst of winter, homework, and snow. One look at them and it was spring again.

Who are these Ambassadors of Happiness? The Beatles—who else? Parents found it hard to believe the four were real, but there they were in all their crowning glory.

I love the Beatles for they are honest boys. Instead of hanging on corners, we listen to their fab recordings. Never is there a dull moment in the life of a Beatlemaniac. Something is always happening. And as I am sure they would put it, "It's all gear, luv."
Patricia T. Gallo, 15
2655 S. Muhlfeld St.

AUGUST 27, 1964
Saw *A Hard Day's Night* for the sixth time at the movies—and now know the dialogue by heart. Some girls were bragging that they saw it twenty times.

Look out, Philly; the Liverpool Lads will soon be here in person!

PLAN B-E-A-T-L-E-S
This is it, our carefully typed memo plan outlining how to meet the Fab Four when they stay in town

47

before the September 2 concert. We each have a role to play and must not goof it up.

1. Rent hotel room at Warwick (save money, four dollars each).
2. Plan ahead how we are going to go about this.
3. Two suitcases and two makeup cases to make it look authentic.
4. Contents: three candy striper uniforms, feather dusters, four sheets, bottle of Pledge, four dust rags, bobby pins, rubber bands, glasses, flat sheets (four pair), small vase with flowers, cake, four letters, and four small presents. Records, letter to them saying we were the maids, small tray. Four good glasses, two bottles of Coke—compliments of the girls in room—bottle opener, homemade cookies, white blouses for uniforms, four old alike aprons (white), hangers, transistor radio, napkins, four plates, forks, one knife, matches, cigarettes one pack only, combs.
5. What to wear when Kathy and Louise come: dresses, gloves, hat, heels, bag. What to wear when Patti, Carol, Nancy come: dress, gloves, hat, heels, and bag.
6. Names: Kathleen O'Hara, Patricia Avillo, Carol and Nancy DeMarco, Louise Boyd.
7. Plan of Action:
   Kathy stays over Patti's house August 31. Brings suitcase August 30 early in morning. Leaves Patti's house about six-thirty, meet Louise at Wanamaker's quarter after seven. Register at Warwick for a night and tell desk clerk you have

48

a couple of friends coming up around nine. Patti calls Kathy's room before she leaves home. Meets Carol and Nancy at Wanamaker's quarter of nine. Arrive at hotel, go in front to desk, Patti asks for Miss O'Hara's room number. Go up to room and change into candy striper uniform complete with apron. While Carol and Patti change (also Louise), Kathy checks halls for guards, police, etc. Eight-thirty Kathy and Louise will explore building to find Beatles' rooms. Kathy changes into uniform.

8. Plans further:

Nancy: Remains in room at all times. Answers the phone and says she is Kathleen O'Hara. MUST NOT LEAVE ROOM. Keep blinds shut. Don't open door to stranger. Code knock is three knocks. Fix room by closing suitcase, etc. Don't lock door!

Louise & Patti: Knock at Beatles' door and say "maid service." (Feather duster and vase with flowers. Patti)

Patti's Job: "Where shall I place the vase? A group of girls gave it to the management and sent it up with us." Dust tables, chairs, etc.

Louise's Job: After she polishes furniture while Patti dusts, she remarks on flowers. She says loudly, "I wonder where Kathy and Carol are. They are supposed to be making the beds." Turns to Beatles, "They are always loafing those two." Five minutes after, Kathy and Carol knock and Patti answers the door. DON'T LAUGH ANYBODY*DO YOU WANT A BEATLE TO KEEP OR NOT!!!! Take time doing your job.

> Kathy & Carol: Enter with sheets and radio—
> under sheets. Play loudly. Two sheets apiece
> and bring letters and presents (from some girls
> outside). Give letters toward leaving time. Kathy
> and Carol in bedroom remark, "My, my, the sheets
> are the wrong size." Turn on radio, start danc-
> ing with the sheets. Strike up conversation with
> "isn't she soft in the head?"
>
> Leave room and bring in tray with Coke, cook-
> ies, and cake.

Gosh, it may or may not be a workable plan, but then, we are not sure the Beatles will stay at the Warwick. Perhaps the plan is way too complicated or incredibly simple. How do we know which day to check in to the hotel? Can you imagine if our folks got wind of what we were doing? It would mean no allowance for a whole year.

Maybe we better hide out at Convention Hall instead.

SEPTEMBER 2, 1964

Kathy and I, camped at the back entrance of Philadelphia Convention Hall, had been waiting forever for John, Paul, George, and Ringo. It was approaching late afternoon. We had arrived at 9:00 A.M. and hidden behind the building before the police assembled the white barricades meant to hold back the thousands of desperate fans sure to swarm around the hall ahead of the 8:00 P.M. concert. In front of the granite building, groups of wide-eyed girls streamed into the area—Beatle business as usual—dressed in casual summer shorts and proudly adorned with Beatle badges. Many of the hopeful fans carried homemade banners proclaiming this the "City of Beatle Love, loyal to Beatles 4-Ever." As I stood squinting in the sunlight, a four-foot-tall sketch of Ringo's face jounced past me, held high by an artistic fan.

Waiting excitedly, we were hip enough not to expect the obvious long, black Cadillac, but neither did we spot the half-expected but telltale delivery van or any other ruse to smuggle the four musicians into the building. All the same, our suspicion grew that they had eluded us, frustrating our one shot at seeing them close up and in the flesh.

As the hours dragged on, Kathy and I were parched, sweaty, and cramped from crouching behind a pillar. Did we dare give up our perch and miss seeing them, arriving stealthily or in a burst of bravado? Unfortunately, our bladders won out, and we melted back over the barricades to join the now twelve thousand fans and police crowding the sidewalks. The ivory marquee announced matter-of-factly, and inaccurately,

TONIGHT
THE BEATLE
HI LIT M.C.
SOLD OUT

Sold out? No kidding. Hy Lit (Hyski), the leading deejay at station WIBG—also known as W-I-Beatle-G—was the champion of the planned Beatles stopover tonight in Philly.

I had the presence of mind to snap a photo of Kathy in front of the marquee with my Instamatic, including some of our school friends all behind the barricades. Everyone was there. Who would miss the Beatles' first concert in Philly?

When they went on sale last May 4, 12,097 tickets sold out in ninety minutes. We were lucky to get tickets, as most fans weren't so fortunate. I bought mine for $5.50 through South Philly "connections" at Nick Petrella's record shop.

Excited screams rose every time a car went by in front of the hall. Word then went out that the group would be smuggled in via truck. Every time a truck passed, the screams grew shrill. By late afternoon, still no Beatles. Sadly, we vacated our post to rush home, dress mod, grab our cherished tickets, and catch the trolley back to Convention Hall.

What to wear to the Beatles concert? I wore my black velvet John Lennon cap, my mod British schoolgirl uniform with tie (matching the attire of Pattie Boyd in the film *A Hard Day's Night*), and lots of Beatle buttons. My most treasured button is shaped like a black plastic guitar featuring a round color photo of Paul's cute face.

There I was again outside Convention Hall: in my hand I held tightly to my light green ticket. Printed on its face: THE BEATLES E U 3 CENTER ORCHESTRA. The concert was wonderful, although I only saw five minutes of it. You see, masses of girls stood on their seats; nobody saw anything! It surely wasn't the Beatles' fault. The show they put on was great! If only I could have seen them or heard them better, it would have been perfect!

Diane hurt her leg when a row of chairs collapsed. How do you balance on the seat of a wobbly folding chair? Everyone was so numb, they just picked up the chairs, stood back on 'em and kept screaming. Once in a while, I could just catch a glimpse of Ringo's drum set way off in the distance under the WIBG radio banner that screamed "A WIBBAGE WELCOME FOR THE BEATLES," but it was hidden by the many figures in front of me, all waving arms and bobbing bodies. The music was drowned out by the girls' voices and the chanting of the four names: "JOHN! PAUL! GEORGE! RINGO!" Every girl in the place demanded individual attention— except for those lucky fans in the first row, who could see Paul smile or even see them sing. Was the music taped? Who knows?

Many of the fans were crying as they shuffled out in shock after the concert. How I landed back home, I don't know. I was sweaty, flushed, and bewildered. My wet hair was plastered to my head under the heavy velvet John Lennon cap. It was over, and I didn't see much of anything. I was so close, yet so far. This was the high point of my young life, but I didn't get to see them, let alone meet Paul. I felt let down and disappointed and thrilled and marvelous all at the same time.

Ah, Paul. I can't stop loving my beloved Paul. I tried, but it's no use. He has some kind of spell over me, and I can't break it! He and I have so much in common. We're both left-handed and have dark hair and brown eyes. When he gets married, he wants a wife who wants a big home in the country. That's exactly what I love. If only I could meet and talk to him. I'd prove to him that I love him for himself and not because he is a Beatle. I love him as a Beatle but as a person first! If only he could know, but I'm just another fan as far as he is concerned. What was the main reason for winning that *Daily News* Beatles essay contest? To maybe meet him, that's why.

It doesn't seem fair that I love someone so much and that people take it for idolism instead of pure love! I have been looking for someone like Paul for a long time, but now that I finally found him, I can't know him. . . . It's just that I would love to talk to him or do the things that he and I like. Our hobbies are similar: photography, drawing, singing, writing (he writes songs—I write anything), and long hair. I would love to walk hand in hand with him. I love him as a person. A person who I need, and I know *he* must need someone: someone maybe like me, who is so similar to him. Maybe he wouldn't love me like I love him, but we should look into this further. I don't scream, for it is juvenile. I don't long for anyone, but I do love him and pray that maybe one day he'll love me.

SEPTEMBER 3, 1964

Footnote to PLAN B-E-A-T-L-E-S. According to a newspaper report, "young femme fans of the Beatles were very much in evidence at the Warwick Hotel, waiting for the arrival of their idols. There was a rumor the Warwick had canceled the Beatles reservation, because of inability to get proper police protection." The manager denied the report, stating that the Warwick is a hotel for show business people and would have never canceled them. "They made the reservations here a month ago. The Liverpool quartet is remaining in Atlantic City and will come direct to Convention Hall from the resort."

SEPTEMBER 5, 1964

The whole town has gone Beatles mad. I mean the William Penn Shop is "honoring the Beatles with this wild cake. C'mon kids! Have a ball with this crazy, but Luscious Pound Cake! M-M-M 2 pounds of tender, delicious butter pound cake, delightfully decorated with chocolate and vanilla butter cream icing." This $1.79 cake is shaped like the head of a Beatle with a mop of chocolate hair and large gooey eyes.

And that's not all.

Even Gimbel's department store is getting into the act. "Yeah! Yeah! Yeah! and now it's a BEATLES MIRROR ready to hang! Overall 19 × 32 inches. Dating for a hard day's night at Convention Hall with John, Paul, George and Ringo? Like you'll scream, screech, and shriek over this beat teen treat in Pittsburgh Plate Glass topped with built-in picture frames and 4 full color photos of the world's wildest 4! Back panel opens . . . change pix at any time, even replace Liverpool's answer to the high cost of haircuts! Dig yours in white, maple or decorator green. And you'll want to hold Gimbel's hand for the hip low price!"

And adults think we Beatlemaniacs are nuts. Beatle albums, magazines, and dolls are a world away from goofy cakes and mirrors.

SEPTEMBER 10, 1964

Well, Robert J. Williams, the Beatle-hating bald writer, is at it again!

An Ice-Cold Performance
Adoring, Well-Behaved Fans Were Short-Changed by Beatles

By ROBERT J. WILLIAMS
Bulletin Amusements Editor

AT THE RISK of shirttail and ear-drum, I went to see The Beatles at Convention Hall last Wednesday night, on the theory that phenomena, such as the Grand Canyon and The Beatles, must be observed in person for one to fully comprehend the awesome spectacle they present.

Well, as reported next day, the familiar ritual of a Beatle appearance was followed precisely on stage and off. The lads sung and were not heard, and the Lolitas out front shrieked and waved frantically, but were not noticed by their idols either as individuals, which was to be expected, or as a mass audience, which ordinary politeness dictates.

The Beatles are a finely-honed fun act, but as cold as a blade of steel. In return for the passionate adulation their followers give them, The Beatles offer no visible appreciation, genuine or make-believe. Their attitude seems almost contemptuous.

• • •

I WOULDN'T BLAME The Beatles one bit for feeling this way, despite the fact that Beatlemania is of their own and their management's making, and that escape with a huge bundle of pounds and shillings can be almost instant: they need only disband the act.

But there can be no excuse, not in my book, anyway, for The Beatles' lack of public manners. Traditionally, performers respond graciously to acclaim, even if the behavior of audiences disgusts them privately — and believe me, I've been ashamed, on numerous occasions, to be part of some audiences.

At Convention Hall, The Beatles came on, went through their well-rehearsed routine, took perfunctory bows, put down their instruments, and walked off. The adoring fans cheered wildly, but there were no curtain calls. It was over and done with, and off to the next engagement.

• • •

IF THE TEENERS and sub-teeners expected more, they certainly didn't so indicate. So blind is the devotion of the typical Beatle fan, I doubt very much that they noticed or cared about amenities. They gave their hearts and their lungs, as previous generations of teeners did for Rudy Vallee and Frank Sinatra. The Beatles didn't bother to toss back a crumb of appreciation.

One other facet of the Beatle session appalled me. It would seem to me that the packagers of their fabulously lucrative U. S. tour could at least have filled out the supporting bill with reasonably competent acts. Not big-name acts, mind you, but performers who might conceivably have made the Ted Mack Amateur Hour. There are good rock'n'roll performers and dreadful ones, you know.

One more thought about Beatles' visit here. The youngsters who came to see them behaved marvelously. Although paralyzed by their adoration, and seemingly oblivious to everything else, they obeyed the safety rules for the most part. When police told them to stop standing on chairs, they got down.

Of course, many of them climbed right back up again, but the point is that these children, most of them, understand discipline, and responded to it despite their frenzy.

This was not a rowdy mob, but good, healthy youth embroiled in uncontrolled adoration. They deserved quite a bit more than they got, at $5.50 a seat.

Oh, Mr. Williams is going to hear from a lot of us in the next few days. His days are numbered. Just wait.

Here is how Jack Helsel of the *Philadelphia Daily News* reviewed the adventures of the Beatles in Philly:

It was a hard day's night for the Beatles, for some 800 cops and hired protectors and for the moptops' thousands of fans—both inside and outside Convention Hall. But nobody seemed to mind that the frantic foursome couldn't be heard because of the shrieks of joy and screams of agony that filled the air the entire half hour the Beatles were on stage.... Either the public address system in Convention Hall wasn't as good as the one in Atlantic City on Sunday, or the 12,037 local teenagers out-yelled and out-squealed the 20,000 plus audience at the shore resort concert.

From the first row in the Hall you could see the Beatles—but you couldn't hear 'em. You couldn't touch 'em either, because 125 cops, Convention Hall guards, ushers and private detectives formed a human wall in front of the stage.

The kids were told to stay in their seats. Some obliged—they stood on their seats. Others sat on their parents' shoulders. And some stood on other kids . . .

The Hard Day's Night actually started yesterday afternoon, as Hy Lit, the WIBG disc jockey, who emceed last night's bash, related to the audience.

The Beatles were smuggled out of their Lafayette Motel room in Atlantic City via a fish delivery truck that transported them to a waiting bus five miles outside the resort town.

They arrived at Convention Hall about 3.51 P.M. yesterday. This was a last minute change in itinerary and washed out a 3 P.M. press party at the Warwick Hotel. But their fans didn't believe it. The Warwick had a mob of 400 girls at 2 P.M. just in case.

At 5 P.M., Moe Septee and Felix Gerstman, promoters of the concert, introduced the "gear guys" to the press who had been summoned to the Hall.

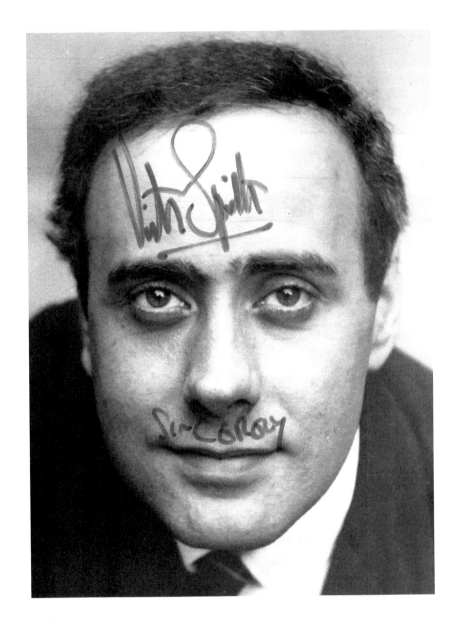

SEPTEMBER 11, 1964

I know this does not seem real, but it is! We became friends with Victor Spinetti. *The* Victor Spinetti, *the* actor who appeared in *A Hard Day's Night*. He played the neurotic TV director and is friends with the Liverpool Lads.

We discovered he was coming to town in Frank Brookhauser's column in the *Philadelphia Evening and Sunday Bulletin,* which announced the American premiere of *Oh What a Lovely War* at the Forrest Theatre on September 14. He said that any true Beatles fan will have found some way to catch the show.

I decided to write personally to Victor at the Bellevue Stratford Hotel, and he *answered*! This is what he wrote:

```
Dear Patricia Gallo,
Thank you for your letter which I received this
morning. You are quite right, we are very busy
with our show but I feel you must have an im-
mediate note from me as you were kind enough to
write; Beatle news cannot wait anyhow.
    They are great fun, very amusing nice people,
very easy to get along with—in short it is not
like work making a film with them. I knew Paul
long before I met the others as he was by way
of being a fan of mine in the show (Oh What A
Lovely War) in London. He has been to parties
at my house and is a fun guest. They joke a lot,
with a particular sense of humor namely Beatle,
partly Liverpool. I met their folks, their par-
ents and their aunts and uncles and they are also
unassuming pleasant, easy to know people. Hard to
believe I know, but all true! They have no angst
whatever and are always a pleasure to meet. In
short, I wish I didn't have to have been nasty
```

to them in the film but someone had to play it. (Success hasn't made them old either.)

O.K. I have to change now and go back to rehearsals. I've enclosed a picture of mine to prove that I am not nasty and unsmiling.

Sincerely,
Victor Spinetti

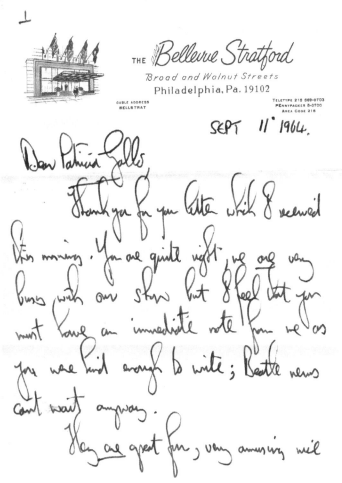

THE *Bellevue Stratford*
Broad and Walnut Streets
Philadelphia, Pa. 19102

CABLE ADDRESS
BELLSTRAT

TELETYPE 215 569-9703
PENNYPACKER 8-0700
AREA CODE 215

SEPT 11 1964.

Dear Patricia Gallo,

Thank you for your letter which I received this morning. You are quite right, we are very busy with our show but I feel that you must have an immediate note from me as you were kind enough to write; Beatle news can't wait anyway.

They are great fun, very amusing well

AIR CONDITIONED GUEST ROOMS, RESTAURANTS AND FUNCTION ROOMS

AUTUMN–WINTER 1964–1965

SEPTEMBER 16-26, 1964

This is the long and short of our week with Victor as we waited after school for him outside the stage door of the Forrest Theatre. He is the nicest and most kindly gentleman and looked so dapper in his blue blazer.

OUR WEEK WITH VICTOR, PART I

Wednesday, September 16: Talked in Mr. Spinetti's dressing room for twenty minutes. Walked him to Bellevue Stratford Hotel.

Saturday, September 19: Gave Victor cake and cookies. Sat in dressing room fifteen minutes. Walked him to Bellevue Stratford.

Monday, September 21: Victor sat and talked with us for ten minutes on step outside theater.

Tuesday, September 22: Talked to Victor at theater, walked him to Bellevue Stratford, and treated us to Coke and milk.

Wednesday, September 23: Met outside the Forrest Theatre and talked and walked to the Bellevue Stratford—and talked with actor Murray Melvin.

Friday, September 25: Victor was rehearsing and very busy. Had decency to come out to say he was very busy, and come back tomorrow.

Saturday, September 26: Walked Victor to hotel and said good-bye. We then bought flowers and rang up room 1524, but no answer. We're in lobby when we saw dear ol' Murray Melvin walk in. We asked for help, and he found Mr. Spinetti—eating. Mr. Spinetti came out of dining room with actress Barbara Windsor. Gave him the flowers and said final good-bye or tah-tah.

OUR WEEK WITH VICTOR, PART II

Our first glimpse of Vic was of him coming through the back exit of the Forrest Theatre where he was rehearsing for *Oh What a Lovely War* on September 16. What we first noticed about this dynamic man was the cute little ski slope of a nose that was perched in the middle of his face. We wanted to talk about how he enjoyed working with the Beatles in *A Hard Day's Night,* and we wanted to find out all about him. Soon we were ushered into his small, air-conditioned dressing room, where we put down schoolbooks, handbags, and the rest of the things most teenage girls carry about with them. Then Victor began to tell us about the "lads" (as he called them), about how he loved the United States and the starring part he had in *Oh What a Lovely War.* We were awestruck as he told us all this but managed somehow to giggle here and there. After talking to him almost a half hour, we walked him to the Bellevue Stratford Hotel. Right then and there, we decided he was such a friendly sort of person that we would like to know him better. We bought tickets to the Saturday afternoon performance and hoped we could see him again. On Saturday, September 19, we saw him before the afternoon performance for a quick minute, and he stated he could see us after the show. We sat through *Oh What a Lovely War* (which was just great) in the balcony with a home-baked cake, chocolate cookies, cameras, tape recorder, etc., and laughed our heads off. When safely in his dressing room, Victor told us how delighted he was that we could make it to see the show. He said he was going to save the cake and cookies till the evening performance and share it with the cast during intermission. We (to say the least) were thrilled and delighted! Again, we made the short trip to the Bellevue Stratford and said good-bye to Mr. Spinetti. Somehow we knew we would be back again to talk to this most interesting British gentleman.

After school on the following Monday, we seemed drawn back to the Forrest Theatre, where they would rehearse every afternoon until about 4:30. While waiting for Victor, we got to know the watchman and found out about his twenty-seven grandchildren. We also got to know the others in the cast. Victor told us about everything under the sun, including his family home, which we found out was in Cwm, South Wales.

We followed Monday's visit with another visit the following day. This time we discussed such important topics as why he didn't want to go to Hollywood. He answered with good wit that he, as an Italian, doesn't like all that sun and tan! Victor was coming down with quite a cold, so on the way back to the hotel, we stopped at Evan's Drug Store on Broad Street for throat lozenges. While in there, he treated us to Cokes, and that's when we spotted a juke box. We played two favorites of ours titled "A Hard Day's Night" and, naturally, "And I Love Her." Victor told us he would never forget when he saw them film the song "And I Love Her." That was his fave from the movie.

On Wednesday, we saw Victor again. When we stopped over on Friday, September 25, we knew he was no ordinary person. This actor was quite busy rehearsing and came out personally to tell us that he would be practicing until curtain time that evening. I don't think many actors would take time out like he did to tell us. We knew that we wanted to do something special for this wonderful person and thought a fan club would be just the thing. We like Victor for himself. When he is onstage or just talking to people, you can see he gives himself freely to everyone. And he loves people.

We saw Victor one more time before he left Philly for New York. That was Saturday, September 26. We went to the Bellevue Stratford with flowers for him and rang up room 1524. When no one answered, we thought for sure we wouldn't hear from him till he was settled in New York. We tried to take the elevator up to his room, but the elevator operator saw we were fans with flowers and would not allow us up. Lurking about in the lobby was Murray Melvin, who heard our sad plight and immediately found Victor in the dining room—lurched him out—and once again we were reunited. He was deeply touched by the flowers, but not as touched as we were by his kindness throughout that week and a half. We knew that he would be hearing a lot from us in the future about the OFFICIAL VICTOR SPINETTI FAN CLUB OF AMERICA.

SEPTEMBER, 29, 1964
We are planning the fan club for Victor. During class, I wrote in my homework assignment book:

```
OFFICERS AND MEMBERS
Diane, President
Patti, President
Jean, Treasurer
Beverly, Secretary
Charter Members: Carol, Ellen, Sue, Mary Anne,
Kathy, Barbara, Dorothy
```

Membership Card: This is to certify that _____ is a member in good standing of the Official Victor Spinetti Fan Club of America, O.V.S.F.C.A. Chapter #1.

OCTOBER 2, 1964

Heard around the halls at school—

```
Eyes of hazel,
Hair of black.
Paul McCartney,
Please come back!
```

OCTOBER 13, 1964

Passed note to Diane:

```
Dear Diane,
Hello. Miss you terribly. I didn't make the
school play. I, myself, did not see the paper
with the names of those girls who got parts, but
Rita saw it and said my name and hers were not
on it. I hope you made it! Denise (you know her,
she's real cute and nice) made it. Oh well, I'm a
failure at fifteen. I really didn't expect to get
in like I said before. Can't wait till school is
over. Meet me by the gate. BRING JUST YOURSELF.
Except if Jean is coming. I'm writing this during
activity period—3rd period.
                                            Patti
```

OCTOBER 18, 1964

Kathy wrote a gear poem about us.

```
TALE OF THREE GIRLS—PATRICIA, CAROL, KATHLEEN
Carol, Carol,
With hair so black,
For you the Beatles will come back,
This we know is a fact,
```

You think about them night and day,
At school, at home, at work, at play,
And these words you always say:
"Give me George, or give me Paul,
It really doesn't matter at all,
Just so one belongs to me,
I love them both can't you see?
And a Mrs. Beatle I hope to be.
Pat, Pat,
Will always be true,
To the Beatle who sings "Till there was you,"
And he is Paul with hair so black,
He smiles sweetly for only Pat,
Her heart is one just for Paul,
He is the Beatle who is six feet tall,
And we know someday they will meet,
And hand in hand walk down the street.
Then comes Kathy hair so brown,
Of the three she is the clown,
Ringo she will never let down,
For he is the new love she has found,
Ringo, Ringo eyes of blue,
Kathy loves only you,
Her eyes twinkle at your name,
She is a real smashing dame.
All three girls love you four,
For good or bad, for rich or poor,
And our love for you has shown,
And every day it has grown and grown,
We three girls, who will be true,
Beatles, Beatles, we love you.

OCTOBER 24, 1964

Diane, Jean, and I went up to New York today by train to see Victor. *Oh What a Lovely War* opened at the Broadhurst Theater on September 30, and we had promised to visit him. Our little group waited by the stage door until he ushered us in after the matinee performance. The next thing I knew, he was whisking us onto the Broadway stage after the show, where we peered out into the empty theater. What a feeling! I felt suspended in time standing on this bare Broadway stage along with Victor. I looked out onto the empty seats where the audience sits, and a chill of excitement went through me. I thought, "Wow, what a moment; I will always remember it." Back in Victor's dressing room, he paid homage to that moment with a glass of champagne—a "bit of the bubbly," he called it. Looking dapper in his brown checked jacket, he turned slightly to toast a poster of the great Marlene Dietrich. This was a dramatic portrait of her face. "IN PERSON DIETRICH" was printed at the bottom. We all felt the electricity.

The three of us talked to Victor about the progress of the fan club. He was pleased. We were surprised to receive glossy autographed photos of the actor and vowed to get up to New York again soon, on another Saturday. He presented each of us with a long-stemmed rose. Before we caught the train back to Philly, we walked him to the Algonquin Hotel. Victor related the history of the famous hotel, which has been the chosen spot for writers, actors, playwrights, and poets for decades.

HERE WAS OUR DAY IN NEW YORK

1. Empire Street
2. Hotel Manhattan Coffee Shop
3. To Broadhurst to meet Spinetti. He said he would see us after show.
4. Walked along Broadway, saw theaters, then hopped a bus and walked along 5th Avenue to UN Building. From UN, went nineteen blocks to Plaza Hotel. Passed St. Patrick's Cathedral and Rockefeller Center. Saw Stage Delicatessen and Sardi's.
5. Went in Spinetti's dressing room, toasted with champagne, and snapped photos. Had our cards hanging up.
6. Walked him to florist shop, where he bought us each a red rose.
7. Walked him to the Algonquin.
8. Then left.

OCTOBER 29, 1964

Bought a copy of October's issue of *Teen Screen* magazine. You will never guess what I found in its pages. They published my poem about Paul! I never imagined I would see it in print with my name at the bottom. Just imagine: *my* poem and *my* name in a national magazine! I had no idea.

No one had contacted me in advance. I opened the magazine, and there it was, in the "Letters to the Editor" section. It is nice to know my "Song of Paul" is now famous. The editor wrote, "Thank you for your poem, Patricia! We sure hope Paul sees it, and since he is a *Teen Screen* fan, he probably will!"

Now I am a published poet.

NOVEMBER 1, 1964

I am very mixed up. I feel as if I want to sing out with joy. But why? Surely this is not a good time to sing out, with a *Latin test* scheduled for tomorrow. I can't help thinking of a happy scene instead of thinking of a *Latin test*. Why am I so happy when I should be miserable, and why am I so miserable at times when I should be happy?

I know it's because of my Jamie (Paul), whom I love beyond recognition.

Guess what? I found copies of the Beatles' autographs in a fan magazine—and spent the entire day at school practicing Paul's signature in between my schoolwork. I got pretty good at it, and now Paul's autograph is all over my copy books. I showed my friends, and they all thought it looked real. Next step is changing the handwritten "P" in my first name "Patti" and substituting Paul's own signature "P" in his first name. So happy we have the same letter in our first names. "Paul and Patti" has a certain ring to it, doesn't it? Well, someday.

NOVEMBER 18, 1964

Things have been moving so fast the past couple of months that I haven't written one word about my new job as a teenage columnist. Believe it or not, the Beatles brought this about in August before their Philly concert. I knew there was no chance to get a press pass from one of the major newspapers in town, so I thought to ask our local weekly *Southwest Philadelphia Globe Times*. I called them up to see if they would like me to cover the concert on September 2. I was extremely polite to their editor. She said the small weekly paper did not receive press passes, but after chatting with me for a while, she had an idea. She asked Diane and me to write a weekly column for teenagers. We could write on anything from music to dating and fads. We call the column *Teen to Teen*, but still no press passes.

Here is our very first column:

Teen to Teen

(Editor's Note: The following article extolling the praises of the Beatles and all the other new groups so dear to the heart of the younger generation, was submitted to the Globe by two local teens—Pat and Diane, both soph-omores at West Catholic. We hope it will fill the "terrible void" in the lives of the dedicated teenagers as their idols fly from country to country. The two teenage reporters plan to submit similar articles regularly. If other fans would like to add or enlarge the column with their own bits of news—let's hear from them.)

The Beatles may be gone from our shores but not from the hearts of many loyal fans (screamies). Their short stay in Philadelphia proved to be a hectic one. Although they were virtually prisoners at Convention Hall, this didn't dull their sense of humor. Ringo Starr, one of the foursome, found his delight before show time in calling the different ticket agencies and anonymously asking if there were any tickets left.

In February the Beatles will begin filming their new movie. The title has yet to be revealed. This film will have more of a plot than *A Hard Day's Night*.

The Dave Clark Five, another top rated group from England, are present-ly touring the U.S. and are due to visit again during the Christmas holidays.

The invasion of many different English singing groups namely: Animals, Rolling Stones, Jerry and Pacemakers, Searchers, Billy J. Kramer, Hollies, Peter and Gordon, etc., has brought back the old traditional rock n' roll to America. Now the American groups, such as the Supremes, are taking over England by complete surprise.

Tomorrow's Top Pops

"Mr. Lonely" by Bobby Vinton is a modern version of the old standard, "She's Not There."

NOVEMBER 22, 1964

I think of a man—tall and handsome—who stands with his beautiful wife and two children. The picture is there, but the true-to-life thing grows dim.

It has been one year ago today that our beloved President John F. Kennedy left our world. In this past year, I haven't thought of him on that last fatal day. Instead, I've thought about him in his happy days. So many times have I seen him with his children: giving Caroline piggyback rides, watching John-John underneath his office desk.

I remember how he and Jackie looked at the Inaugural Ball. As one reporter put it, "they looked like a football hero and his beautiful date going to the senior prom."

Although he is gone forever, we will never forget this man who gave his life for our country; this man who was a husband, father, and great president; this man who was loved by all, except one who stood by a warehouse window with a telescopic rifle.

DECEMBER 1, 1964

Ringo's tonsils were removed today at the University College Hospital in London. We all spent anxious hours in front of the radio waiting for news of the operation. Poor Kathy was a wreck, but she seems to be OK. And so is Ringo.

To cheer Kathy up, I bought her a copy of the latest 16 *Magazine.* I bet she will enjoy reading: "16 invites you to visit the homes of the Beatles. C'mon along to hear what their parents and relatives have to say about them." "Introducing the Animals." "The 3 wild lives of Elvis."

DECEMBER 10, 1964

Two years have flown by since the first entry into my journal. Two years today. I ask myself, in these two years, have I grown up much? I believe I have. I have grown in spirit. I hope I am a little less foolish in some things, and in other ways, I think I have grown wiser. Of course, in other areas, I have grown happier as I have followed the Beatles. Two years have slipped by as if a day. I hope to write even after I am old and gray. Cheerio!

DECEMBER 18, 1964

Diane and I had our very first interview today. We called radio station WIBG to ask if leading deejay Hy Lit was available. We told them we were columnists who wrote *Teen to Teen* for a small local paper. Although the secretary had not read about us, she gladly set up an interview with

Hy Lit himself. Today we went to the radio station, met "Hyski," and interviewed him for *two hours.* Hy Lit looked great in a dark blue shirt, black vest, and dark straight pants. His hair was slicked back, a bit like Elvis's, although he reminded me of Frankie Avalon. He was so kind and interested in what we asked him. Of course, we asked a lot about the Beatles, as he met them in September when he was MC at the concert. You can tell he really understands teenagers, even though he has not been one for some years. He really knows his rock music, too. We came right back home and were so excited that we wrote the column immediately. Wish we were as eager to do our homework.

The article will appear mid-January—with a bit of editing, I am guessing.

DECEMBER 22, 1964

A mop of dark, rich brown hair, two black button eyes, a cute turned-up nose, a strong build, and a great personality make up my Jamie (Paul). I read an awful rumor about him today and hope it is not true. Give me the strength not to believe it! It is a horrible rumor.

I spotted the *Midnight* tabloid newspaper at the train station coming home from school and its glaring headlines about Paul. The cover screamed, "Beatle Fathers Illegitimate Baby. the World Exclusive Story and Photo." We never buy those newspapers in the Gallo household, but I did today. I felt nasty sneaking it back home. On page 8 was the headline "Paul McCartney is the father of my child—A Midnight Exclusive." The article itself told of a nineteen-year-old Liverpool girl who had given birth to Paul's baby nine months ago.

Can you imagine?

Well, anyway, a Merry Christmas to everyone. I wish we had mistletoe so we could put some up, and then I wish the Beatles would visit me!

I see a green hill in a dream. It is misty, but I can see someone tall and majestic at the top waiting for me. The road up this hill is a long, steep one, but eventually I'll get to that tall figure on the very top. Only time will tell!

DECEMBER 22, 1964

Teen to Teen

By Diane & Patricia

First of all, we would like to wish a very Merry Christmas to everyone from: The Animals, Beatles, Beach Boys, Beau Brummels, Bachelors, Cilla Black, Chuck Berry, Candy and the Kisses, Chad & Jeremy, Petula Clark, Dave Clark Five, Dolphins, Drifters, Everly Brothers, Four Seasons, Fourmost, Gestures, Gerry & the Pacemakers, Herman's Hermits, Hollies, Hullaballoos, Impressions, Jan and Dean, Kinks, Billy J. Kramer, LuLu and the Lovers, Mersey Beats, Manfred Mann, Marvelettes, Nashville Teens, New Beats, Roy Orbison, Peter and Gordon, Elvis Presley, Pretty

Things, Tommy Quickly, Righteous Brothers, Rolling Stones, Ripcords, Searchers, Supremes, Shangri-Las, Dusty Springfield, Tymes, Tams, 4 Tops, Ventures, Waikikis, You Know Who Group, Zombies, oh—and us!

The Christmas Season has spurred us to transform an old "Christmas Standard" to modern day lingo. Here it is: "Ringo the Big Nosed Beatle"— to the tune of "Rudolph the Red Nosed Reindeer."

Ringo the Big Nosed Beatle had a gigantic nose. And if you ever saw it, you would even say it glows. All of the other Beatles used to laugh and call him dumb. Then one foggy Liverpool night—John Lennon came to say, "Ringo with your drums so gear—sit in with us so all can hear." Then how the Beatles loved him, as they shouted out with glee, "Ringo the big nosed Beatle—you'll go down in history."

A nice Christmas present to Elvis Presley from Ed Sullivan for performing on his show for twenty minutes is two million dollars.

Beatle John Lennon has signed to take part in a new fortnightly review titled "Not Only . . . But Also," starting January 9 he'll read his own poems and appear in a film sequence.

Christmas Top Pops: "The Man With All the Toys," by the Beach Boys, "Do You Hear What I Hear?," by Bing Crosby, "I Saw Mommy Kissing Santa Claus," by the Four Seasons, and "Winter Wonderland," by Darlene Love and the Crystals. These are all new renditions which seem to be catching on in this part of the country.

Special to all our readers: This past Saturday, we had the privilege to have a private interview, which lasted for two hours, with the famed WIBG deejay Hy Lit. There is lots to tell about so until then may we borrow those immortal words of Hy Lit and say, "Keep a cool paw, live, love, laugh and be happy."

DECEMBER 27, 1964

Christmas is even better this year since they have been playing the Beatles' Christmas message on the radio. The Lads record a special end-of-the-year greeting for their fan club. All four of them take a turn to speak and send their thanks, joke around, and sing. I scribbled down some things they said.

DECEMBER 30, 1964

Take a look at our very special holiday column:

Teen to Teen

By Diane & Patricia

Happy New Year to all our loyal readers. Here's a little ditty that might brighten up your Holiday Season:

LIVERPOOL CHRISTMAS

Trim the tree with us today,

Our visitors come from Liverpool way.

Bring the tinsel and tree shaped like a cone,

And don't forget to take along the Rolling Stones.

Of course our guests of honor are John, George, Ringo and Paul,

With them the tree trim party will be a ball.

Along with the Beatles comes Brian Epstein—the boss,

Following them to see they aren't at a loss.

Here comes Dave Clark with the gear tree,

So big it stands—even Tommy Quickly can see.

Cilla Black, Dusty Springfield & Petula Clark are there

Dressed in their best,

You can see plainly they don't want to get messed.

But Peter and Gordon are right there pitching in,

I wonder if anyone invited Peter Asher's next of kin?

Billy J. Kramer seems to mount the ladder with care,

It's a wonder he could see because of his hair.

Chad and Jeremy have been eating all day,

I wonder how much refreshments those two packed away?

Gerry and his Pacemakers are putting on the last ball,

Actually Gerry never seemed very tall.

But the final touches lie in the star,

Which will be put on top by one loved from afar.

Up the ladder—carefully but slowly—what a sight,

Ringo puts on the star and somehow that seems right.

JANUARY 2, 1965

My Christmas presents were gear this year. Under the tree were some really neat clothes, a winter scarf and matching black-and-white wool John Lennon cap, books, a Beatles charm bracelet, perfume, and a mod Christmas dress. A total surprise from Santa was *The Beatles Story,* an album featuring actual interviews with the Liverpool Lads. One thing was missing: the newly minted *Beatles '65* album. All in time, Patti, all in time . . .

JANUARY 3, 1965

What do our parents think of us going nuts over the Beatles? Naturally, it is different from one household to the next. In my own case, Mom says she used to swoon over Frank Sinatra so this is nothing new to her. I think they called themselves "bobby-soxers," listened to Frankie on the radio, and flocked to his special appearances. Today Sinatra plays Las Vegas and stars in films, but back then he was a teenage idol. Mom knows where I am coming from. She feels I am "safe" if I follow the Beatles, as they are far away in England and pose no threat to us. It is not as if I had a giant crush on a guy down the block and was parking with him at the drive-in and drinking wine on the weekends. My dad is neutral on the subject of the Beatles. He hands over my allowance for me to buy records, posters, magazines, and assorted Beatles junk. I can't imagine what crush *he* had as a lad, but I seem to recall battalions of soldiers during World War II carried their Betty Grable pinups to the front lines.

Nothing really changes.

Sadly, I do have friends at school whose parents forbid them to get involved with "this Beatle thing." These girls cannot understand why their parents, especially their dads, are so unbending. They are not allowed to buy Beatles records or wear Beatles buttons. Now this is tragic, because if you don't have zany fun like this when you are fifteen, when can you?

Within our group, Diane is allowed the most freedom to be a Beatles fan. Her bedroom is decorated in early Beatles, including the walls and ceiling. Her friends and the music are warmly welcome. Diane is always the first to buy the new albums. We love to congregate at her place, as it is so inviting. All in all, it is a great place to feel a part of the Beatles.

JANUARY 6, 1965

I am not one who can wait for anything, at least that is what my mom says about me. I said farewell to my Christmas money when I stopped by Jolly's Record Store. *Beatles '65* was looking too good to pass up. This cover is so fab. To portray 1965, the Beatles pose in four different seasonal scenes on the cover. On top, they all sit in suits under large English umbrellas. This is winter. Below, they play with large springs in their hands for spring, naturally. Next, John sits under a big umbrella while the other Lads make like it is a summer heat wave. Lastly, autumn is portrayed as the four sweep up what look like leaves into a basket. Ringo wears a boss black turtleneck, and George looks gear in a pink shirt.

About the music, I must admit that some of the songs were not exactly to my taste. "Mr. Moonlight" and "Baby's in Black" were my least favorite. I do love the rest, especially "I'll Be Back," "I'll Follow the Sun," "Rock and Roll Music," "She's a Woman," and "I Feel Fine." The haunting melody of "I'll Be Back" really appeals to me for some reason. "I'm a Loser" is so very sad. Don't the Beatles have it all? How can they possibly write about being a loser in love? Never happen.

JANUARY 9, 1965

Kathy has made both the *Philadelphia Daily News* and the *Philadelphia Inquirer* newspapers! She even got her picture in the *Daily News*. Kathy and some of her Beatle friends wrote to Philadelphia's mayor James H. J.

Tate to suggest "a corps of young female Bobbies to protect the Beatles" the next time they performed in Philadelphia. Kathy sent a number of letters to the mayor and said that the Bobbies "would make the visit less hectic and release policemen for more important duties."

Well, Mayor Tate shot Kathy down by saying, "Who is to carry away the faintees? Are you young ladies strong enough?" He thought the girls should have the police protect the Beatles "while you protect the police" by persuading "your schoolmates and friends to behave like the young ladies you are."

Of course, Kathy was not thrilled with the mayor's response. She told the journalists that "I was very honored to receive his letter, but I disagree with him."

She said, "Our idea for the Beatle Bobbies wasn't to replace *all* the police. You'd still need some to carry out anyone who fainted, but we could assist the police. A Bobbie corps was formed in Baltimore, and 250 girls participated. The officials said it was a big success. How can it work in Baltimore and not in Philadelphia?"

The mayor also came up with an idea that did not make any of us happy. "Maybe the Beatles' next visit can be postponed for a long, long time," he said.

Good thing I can't vote.

Good for Kathy, too. You got to hand it to her. She put up a good fight.

Kathy got great headlines: "Tate Bans Bobbies for Beatle Guards" and "Beatle Buffs' Bold Bluff Backfires."

Never underestimate the power of Beatles fans. We are the ones with integrity to write nasty letters to nasty newspaper people who say nasty things about the Lads. We enter every Beatle contest we can find, make ourselves known to columnists, and compose Beatle poetry for fan magazines. And that is only the beginning.

Here is a typed reply I received from the *Evening and Sunday Philadelphia* TV critic after he panned the Beatles:

Dear Reader:

May I take this means to thank you for your letter about The Beatles. Yours was one of many hundreds received. While I would like to answer each one individually, this will acknowledge that your comments have been received and read with a great deal of interest, not only by me but by others of *The Bulletin* staff.

    Respectfully,

    Rex Polier

    Television Critic

JANUARY 13, 1965

Finally, our column on Hy Lit appeared in the *Southwest Globe Times.*

Teen to Teen

By Diane & Patti

In answer to the inevitable question, "What is a Hy Lit?" as asked by the Beatles and others, we would like to try to answer this.

Hy Lit was born in Philadelphia on May 20. He attended the University of Miami, where he majored in dramatics. After the countless MC'ing of many different radio and TV programs he finally settled down at WIBG. Because of his good looks and warm personality, he is affectionately called HYSKI. In our talk with him, we asked many thought provoking questions.

To the question, "What do you think of teenagers in general?" he answered: "I am 100% for the kids; I don't cater to adults who say I'm playing garbage. But to teenagers I'd give three days, to adults—three seconds."

He has a lot of patience with teens, and tries to convert the wild ones by talking reason to them.

When asked about his record hops, he replied that he has the most fun doing them. He usually walks out into the crowds and talks to as many teens as he possibly can. He said, "As long as I can do them, I will."

Standing on the stage with the Beatles and getting an ovation as big as they did, was one of his greatest thrills. Although being the number one DJ seems to be just as big. Adult listeners seem to outnumber the teenagers; this too is one of his great thrills.

Hy mentioned that he likes to cook and fix things. Most of all, he enjoys making Caesar salads. He could spend hours fixing something, and then in the end throw it away. Because of his tight schedule, he has little time for hobbies.

His dislikes are few. He hates the sly little people in stores who say, "Come back and see us again sometime." And also adults, who ask if he likes that junk that he plays.

On nicknames, he stated that in his old neighborhood everyone had either "rooney" or "ski" on the end of their names. Thus he acquired "HYSKIOROONEY."

He says from the heart, "I more than appreciate the many fans that I have, and thank everyone for making me the No. 1 DJ in Philadelphia."

For more than three years he has been No. 1, and is extremely charming and intelligent. Incidentally, he is married to the former Miriam Uniman and they have a son, who is seven years old.

Hyski does tremendous charity work for the "DELAWARE VALLEY TEENAGE MERCY CHAPTER OF THE CITY OF HOPE" . . . and during the Christmas season is especially active in this field.

Hy Lit, YOUR MAN ABOUT MUSIC, is an extraordinary human being, having all the qualities of an all-American DJ, and in our opinion, Hy should get an award for being the top disc jockey in the country. And remember, "KEEP A COOL PAW, LIVE, LOVE, LAUGH AND BE HAPPY, AND DON'T BE NOBODY'S FOOL—YA' DIG? SOLID TED, 'NOUGH SAID."

JANUARY 18, 1965

Believe it or not, this is the night before exams and there is not a nervous bone in my body. You heard it right—I'm a changed girl!

I guess I did I tell you that I got *both* albums: *The Beatles Story* double album and *Beatles '65*? *The Beatles Story* tells the history of the group with interviews and songs. It is OK, but not my favorite at all. Now *Beatles '65* is a whole other story. As I mentioned, I just love "I'll Follow the Sun," "I'll Be Back," "She's a Woman," "I Feel Fine," and "Rock and Roll Music." The music really wakes you up and makes you forget about your Latin test.

FEBRUARY 10, 1965

Well, back to the humdrum school world. Yes, school, day in and day out, and no holidays (save weekends) since Christmas! Two months without a breather—five days a week. Wow. What keeps me going? Music—in the form of the Beatles, gear groups, records, singing, and guitar playing. That's me, jack of all trades.

Weather should be breaking in a few weeks, though. All in all, it hasn't been too bad a winter so far. If we only had one snow day off though—I'd be happy.

Teen to Teen

By Patti & Diane

Victor Spinetti, the delightful actor who played the impatient director in *A Hard Day's Night* has agreed to perform in the next Beatle production. Spinetti leaves from London to New York for consultations for the movie, and on Wednesday he will fly to the Bahamas with the Beatles to start filming. Incidentally, the movie will be filmed in the Bahamas, Austria, and England.

FEBRUARY 12, 1965

REFLECTIONS
It was just a year today,
We teens laid our cares away.
To follow the eternal call,
Of gear John, George, Ringo and Paul.
We came with them through thick and thin,
We stuck with them all out and all in.
Never did we have such a ball,
As through Spring, Winter, Summer and Fall.
And I know the story will be told and retold,
How all of their countless records had sold.
We the fans will remember when we're old,
This part of life was meant to cherish and hold.
    -Patricia T. J. Gallo

Earlier tonight, I saw the Beach Boys in person at Convention Hall. It was a fab concert—and wish it would not have ended. We are writing more about the Beach Boys in our *Teen to Teen* column.

FEBRUARY 17, 1965
Can you believe it? Victor sent us the wonderful fuzzy sweater he wore in the movie *A Hard Day's Night*. We were so excited that we smelled it to get a whiff of Victor, John, Paul, George, and Ringo. Immediately we contacted Jack Helsel, who is the *Teen Scene* columnist over at the *Philadelphia Daily News*. He interviewed us, and a picture of Victor wearing the V neck sweater in the film appeared in the paper today on page 25.

Teen Scene: *Beatle's Buddy Gives Gals Wrap*

By Jack Helsel

Next to owning a sweater worn by a Beatle, the best bet for a Beatlemaniac is to hold a sweater worn by a Beatles' buddy.

Like the prize possession of five West Catholic Girls High students that was actually touched (EEEEEK) by all four of the moptops.

The five gals are the hierarchy of the Victor Spinetti Fan Club. Spinetti, a personable young actor who starred with the Beatles in *A Hard Day's Night,* sent them the big black mohair wrap that he wore in the movie.

Fan club co-president Pat Gallo, 15, and Diane Lamont, 16, met Spinetti (who played the nervous TV director in the Beatles flick) when he was in Our Town last year with the musical, *Oh What a Lovely War.*

They were so impressed by him that they organized the fan club, corresponded with him in New York, etc. He was due to visit the gals at their homes and meet their parents last week, but Beatle business came up.

Spinetti called Diane to tell her he had to leave for the Bahamas, locale for the next movie of the Liverpool lads. But added the actor, "I'm sending you a present—it's something that's been touched by all the Beatles."

The sweater arrived last week and Diane's been carrying it to school daily. "It's very big, comes down to my knees," she giggled. Pat starts wearing it today, and then it will be rotated to the other three officers of the VS fan club.

Teen to Teen

By Patti & Diane

Well, it finally happened, another Beatle took the short stroll to the altar. Ringo Starr at 8:15 (British time) on Thursday, February 11 at Caxton Hall in London married Maureen Cox. Maureen was a hairdresser, and has known Ringo since he became a Beatle. At the 5-minute ceremony, those in attendance were: Brian Epstein, as best man; the bride's parents and Ringo's parents; Mr. J.W. Lennon and wife; and one G. Harrison. At the end of the ceremony, John Lennon got a bit carried away and when Ringo solemnly stated "I DO," Lennon applauded. The bride and groom had a short honeymoon in a seaside resort near London. We send our congratulations to the happy couple. Well girls, two down and two to go!

The above appeared in our column today, but the truth of the matter is we had a rough day at school with Kathy, our biggest Ringo fan. She was crying in the locker room in the morning, shaking her head in disbelief that Ringo could do such a thing to her. Ringo really is the love of her life. Kathy was so upset, but we tried to pull her together before the homeroom bell rang. It was bad for Grace, too. She was in so much pain that she could hardly speak. I wonder if Ringo's framed photo will get tossed out of her handbag?

A word about Beatle girlfriends and wives: it's a love/hate relationship. We really love Cynthia and baby Julian. Cynthia has been there forever at John's side. Actress Jane Asher, who is beautiful and sophisticated, is Paul's love—and we don't like her. George's blonde model girlfriend Pattie Boyd met him on the set of *A Hard Day's Night*. She is not our favorite either. Why? Who knows? We feel that these bachelors belong to the world and to us in particular. We *are* young, have secret visions of marrying our heartthrobs, and making every other girl on this planet envious. Now, Ringo is married, and personally I don't feel one way or the other about his Maureen. In fact, this whole girlfriend and wife thing makes me irritated.

FEBRUARY 24, 1965

Teen to Teen

By Patti & Diane

The Beatles' new movie *A Talent for Loving* will not be released until this summer. But here is a little preview:

A very expensive diamond ring is stolen, and it pops up in Ringo's room. The others start to distrust him, but find that he wasn't the culprit.

There is a girl and a love story involved, but the director has yet to name the lucky Beatle.

Paul Anka has become the continental king. He lives in Paris and New York, buys his clothes in England and Italy, gets his shoes from Spain, and has a wife from Egypt.

Chad & Jeremy have been making it big lately, with the filming of TV shows and the release of a new record, so here are a few facts about them. Chad Stuart was born 21 years ago in Windermere, England. He was educated at the Durham School, followed by study at the Art School and Sorbonne in Paris. He joined a publishing house as a copyist and arranger to help his musical ambitions.

Jeremy Clyde was born 22 years ago at Buckinghamshire, England. He was educated at Eton, and had a formal education at Grenoble in France. While there he studied Speech & Drama, and played in a rock-n-roll group during his spare time for two years. Jeremy is very modest and hides the fact that he is the grandson of the Duke of Wellington.

Both met about a year ago at a party, started talking music, and found their views on the subject the same. Their first record was "Yesterday's Gone" which introduced the "Oxford Sound" to the American public.

The Beach Boys are the latest things in America since the introduction of the surfboard. At Convention Hall in Philly on Friday the 12th of February, they proved that surfing music is still regarded high on the lists of American teens. They themselves arrived late, due to fog conditions, but were worth the waiting for. Many of the songs they sang were "golden" records they had recorded in the past. Pandemonium broke out when drummer Dennis Wilson threw one of his drumsticks into the audience. The Beach Boys used much of the idea of audience participation in their concert, and with much success. All in all, it was a great evening and we hope there will be more of these teenage shows in Philly.

Tomorrow's Top Pops

With the record-breaking success of her last hit—"Downtown," Petula Clark will no doubt be contending for the top spot again. This time her new record is about the famous Cavern in Liverpool. It's called "I Know a Place." The Animals haven't had a hit since "The House of the Rising Sun," which was No. 1 during the summer. "Don't Let Me Be Misunderstood" is their new single and surely compares to their first chart-buster.

Last week's Mystery Personality was Bobby Rydell.

Mystery Personality of the Week: I have never been popular here in the U.S., but my records have been number one in England. I was born in Texas, and have very long hair. I've appeared on TV shows here. Who am I? Send all entries to Diane.

MARCH 3, 1965

NOW WE GOT THEIR AUTOGRAPHS!!!!!!! Courtesy of Victor, they just arrived at my house. We are so thrilled that we wrote about it in our *Teen to Teen* column, and we called Jack Helsel over at the *Philadelphia Daily News.*

Teen to Teen

By Diane & Patti

Our non-secret agent 008–1/4 Victor Spinetti, who is traveling with the Beatles, has sent the officers of his fan club a menu. It is just like any other menu, except for the fact that it came with the Beatles from London, and has their autographs on the back of it.

And Jack Helsel wrote in the *Philadelphia Daily News*:

Beatle Bits

Latest local Beatlegacy is a BOAC airlines menu signed by all four of the Liverpool lads while en route to the Bahamas for their new flick, "Beatles Two." The menu is in the proud possession of West Philly fillies Diane Lamont and Patti Gallo, who tell us Lennon and McCartney are rewriting the movie script as the cameras roll.

Mr. Helsel also wrote this about us last month when he made us his *Teen Scene* column correspondents:

The two new "Teen Scene" correspondents from West Catholic High School for Girls are Pat Gallo and Diane Lamont. The 15-year-olds are columnists in a West Philadelphia weekly; specialize in Beatle banter and "exclusives" they get from British pen pals.

Back to the autographs: I am actually touching something that the Beatles' held in their own hands! The menu is from their transatlantic chartered BOAC plane from London. It truly is THE BEATLES BAHAMAS SPECIAL and offers an assortment of foods as they flew to their destination. Victor wrote to us inside the front cover, and the Beatles *all* signed the menu on the white back cover.

Let me describe in detail this most incredible gift of all gifts from our Victor.

The cover of the menu is turquoise, orange, and green, and on it is printed:

BOAC—CUNARD

MENU

Services operated by BOAC—Cunard by BOAC

On the inside front cover, Victor wrote:

For All at Philly

Love

Victor Spinetti

At Present Working

On Beatles Two!

See Back Page for

Autographs of the 4 Lads

Page One:

BOAC CUNARD

Welcomes you aboard this flight

***

BEATLES BAHAMAS SPECIAL

**

London—New York

February, 1965

Page Two:

Cocktails & Iced Fruit Juices

Gin Mixes

Wines from the Vineyards of Bordeaux and the
Cote d'Or

Champagne Cordon Rouge Brut

Whiskies: Scotch * Canadian * American

Continental Lager * English Beer

A further choice is available at your request.

Page Three:

Cocktail Service

Hot and Cold Canapes

LUNCH

Fresh Seafood with Cocktail Sauce

*

Clear Turtle Soup Amontillado

*Filet of Beef with Button Mushrooms

Buttered Vegetables

New Potatoes Rissolees

*Gateau Mille Feuille

*

English and Continental Cheeses

Cream Crackers

*

Fresh Fruits

*

Coffee

Page Four:

Afternoon TEA

Assorted Finger Sandwiches

*

French Pastries

*

Almond Cake * Sweet Biscuits

*

Tea with Milk or Lemon * Coffee

On the inside back cover:

We hope that you have enjoyed your journey and that
we will have the pleasure of your company again.

89

Back Cover:

Paul McCartney
(signed in pencil)

John à Lennon
(in pencil with French à)

Ringo Starr
(in pen and flourishing a star under his
signature)

George Harrison
(signed in pen)

Each autograph is about one inch high. Words cannot express how we feel right now. Victor is so incredible! This is such an honor.

MARCH 10, 1965
And the big headlines in my March issue of 16 *Magazine*: "Cynthia's Secret—How to Hold Your Guy" (the example set by Cynthia Lennon as she is gentle, and not moody, has taste, is loyal and patient). "Jane Asher's Rise to Stardom in Pix." "Be Beatle People."

"Ringo's Hates & Loves"
- I hate to be away from my drums very long.
- I love big parties that really swing.

SPRING-SUMMER 1965

Teen to Teen

By Patti & Diane

NEWS FLASH! NEWS FLASH! Our secret agent with the Beatles, 008 1/4, Victor Spinetti, has done it again. Detouring from Austria en route back to England, the Fab Four, the Beatles, will be having a secret rendezvous and interview with yours truly. So tune in next week and get all the gear facts and story from your Teen to Teen nutnicks.

Everybody's getting married today, and Gerry Marsden (Gerry and the Pacemakers) is no different. His longtime fan club president, Pauline Beehan, who is 21, will be the new Mrs. Marsden.

When John Lennon tried skiing for the first time in Switzerland, his instructor, Hans Hass, said, "Mr. Lennon is quite a good pupil and did good the first time out." Said John, "It's a bit of all right. I'll go on again tomorrow. I'll get this if it kills me." Watch your step, dear John.

Here are a few new groups which will soon be taking the pop music field by storm. The Byrds, The Gonks, Wayne Fontana and the Mindbenders, Georgie Fame and the Blue Flames, The Applejacks, and The Fourpennies.

The famous agent 007 Aston Martin type of car seems to be catching on. Paul McCartney owns a blue one, but George Harrison had to get into the act and bought a white one.

Actress Jane Asher of England has been made a permanent member of a British Broadcasting show. Answering questions and giving advice is her new job.

Charlie Watts of the Rolling Stones has written a book entitled *Bird*. It is about the life of the late and great Charlie "Bird" Parker, who was a jazz saxophonist.

Terry Black, who is sometimes called the Elvis Presley of Canada, is recording on Tollie records. His new release, "Can't We Go Somewhere" will soon be tearing up the charts.

A bright new singing star fresh out of (you guessed it) England is called Twinkle. She writes and sings all her songs, and her newest song "Terry" didn't have what it takes. Oh well, there was never a twinkle yet that wasn't a star.

Last week's Mystery Personality was Cilla Black. We were just overcome with all the correct entries.

Mystery Personality of the Week: This is really going to be hard this week, so good luck. I get my name from four things that I wear on my fingers. I am distinguished from the others by my large "trombone hooter." I also play the drums. Who am I? Send all entries to Diane.

Beatle Bits

When the Beatles landed in Austria they were greeted by 5,000 screaming girls carrying picket signs. Seems they want our lads to go back to England. Don't worry though for there always is the U.S.

Our Secret Agent 008 ¼ has done it again. Mr. Spinetti sent the officers of his fan club some things very dear to the hearts of any Beatle luver. Seems they now own a cigarette smoked by none other than John Lennon. Also a drink stirrer with the inscription "Balmoral Club— Nassau Bahamas" used by Paul McCartney. Also there were two little blue candles used on George Harrison's birthday cake.

Paul admits that "We are all telly addicts watching anything from Andy Pandy and the Wooden Tops to the news in Welsh."

And for all those people who have been writing to us for the addresses of the Lads, here are two of them:

Mr. & Mrs. J. W. Lennon
"Kentwood"
Cavendish Road
St. Georges Hill
Weybridge
Surrey, England

And

Mr. G. Harrison
Fairmille Estates
Wall Bungelow
Claremont, Esher
Surrey, England

Ta-ra till next week.

Yes, Victor has done it again. This is unbelievable. I just opened a package he sent with personal souvenirs while on location with the Beatles. We now own one Peter Stuyvesant cigarette butt smoked by none other than John Lennon. Also, one drink stirrer with the inscription "Balmoral

Club—Nassau Bahamas," used by Paul McCartney, was in the package. We also found two wonderful blue candles that topped George Harrison's birthday cake. Exciting, isn't it? Can you picture Victor grabbing those candles when no one was looking? Jean could not believe they sat on George's very own cake.

Naturally, we returned the favor. We sent Victor some things to give the Beatles. We stopped in town at one of the tiny shops where you can make an instant record. Somehow Diane, Jean, Barbara, and I sang on key and sent off our record entitled "Batto and Her Monsters." We also forwarded Victor Spinetti Fan Club membership cards, as they asked to join our club for Victor. He wrote back to us to say that John, Paul, George, and Ringo, and even their manager Brian Epstein, are now proud members of his club. Can you imagine! In our letters to Victor, we have hinted that we plan on getting to England just as fast as we can somehow to camp on the Beatles' doorsteps.

APRIL 24, 1965

Everyone has been talking about the movie *My Fair Lady,* so we decided to dress up and go into town to see it. I wore last week's Easter outfit. This is my first really grown-up dress. It is a long-sleeved navy blue silk form-fitting dress with a white lace ruffled front and white lace cuffs. I just love it. Wearing it makes me feel older than fifteen. I feel absolutely sophisticated. It has a wonderfully mod look about it, too.

The movie was playing at the Stanley Theatre at 19th and Market Streets. I paid a whopping $2.30 for my ticket. Audrey Hepburn was great as Eliza Doolittle, but I would have enjoyed seeing Julie Andrews play the role in the film. The costumes and music made everything so elegant and British. I must ask my parents for the LP as a birthday present.

Speaking of elegance and mod styles, what has been popular here are knee-high leather boots to wear with new shorter skirts—fashioned after the mod (modern) or Chelsea looks originating from London. Some of these fashion items from England are really expensive and could take a really big chunk out of Dad's salary. The best things to buy are more reasonably priced fashions made in the United States but that copy the new British fashion.

We now write and distribute a newsletter to the members of our fan club. It is hard work, but we need to get the news out about Victor and the Beatles.

APRIL–MAY NEWSLETTER

O.V.S.F.C.A. NEWS FOR YOU

HELLO Here we are back again to bring you up to date on our favorite.

Plenty of adventure has busied Victor since our last news sheet. You may have heard he is playing a very big part in the new Beatle movie, *Eight Arms to Hold You.* Ah, what will become of our hero this time? Maybe he's to play the jolly old London detective with a pipe and Sherlock Holmes cap; or even better yet how about one of the boys' aunts? All wrong. I hope your hair doesn't turn to Brillo and your nose turn up like a ski slope, but our handsome, distinguished English young gentleman has turned out to be a MAD SCIENTIST. Can't you just see it now: Victor running around in a long white lab coat, big bubbly eyes waiting to experiment with a guinea pig and to top it off a sly villainous laugh to express his complete satisfaction in changing Paul McCartney into a thumb-like creature? Ah ha ha. Why Paul the victim? Who knows what happens in this mad picture. As far as we know the plot goes as follows: A ring has been stolen from a museum and the police have worked up their dandruff trying to get a lead on it. The one and only Ringo Starr has it in his possession and this poor innocent flower has no idea how it got there. Now our good little boy scout returns it to the police *thinking* to clear himself completely. He may be good at convincing women like Maureen Starr, but he's certainly no expert with the male sex. No one believes him including the other stars John, Paul and George. Somewhere this beautiful girl named Eleanor Bron comes into the picture and turns out to be the heroine for our boys. In the meantime we imagine Victor has something to do with this ring and the fact is we have a (PAUL MCCARTNEY) and four Ringos running

95

around. Don't ask for an explanation, we haven't received one of them yet. Actually we hate to keep you in suspense by not finishing the story but that is where we are now. You'll have to wait until the fab movie comes out to tie everything up.

WHERE THEN; WHERE NOW

I guess you are all wondering what has become of Victor, where he is and has been and all that sort of thing.

Well formerly in the Bahamas for four weeks, he gained a lot of fab tan of which we were all jealous, and after the Bahamas he left for Austria on March 11. There he continued filming on the ski slopes of the frigid region, but don't worry. One of his club branches came through and sent him a gorgeous blue plaid scarf which I am sure he will wear even to the beach. Presently he is in London, his home. Shooting will continue at Twickenham Studio and on London streets.

NEWSPAPER TO THE AUTHORS

You may wonder where we get all our info and why *most* of it is *almost* completely correct. Well along with Vic's constant correspondence we have other branches of Victor Spinetti Fan Clubs scattered all over as well as in England. Just to name a few there is a fab one in New York, outside of New York we find Chicago, Illinois and we are proud to say these busy bees made it their business to be the plaid scarf senders. The big firm or the first and official club of Victor Spinetti is in where else London, England. These girls are responsible mostly for the life history of our boy which is extensive.

If any of you have friends or relatives who wish to join, have them write to us.

MORE THEATRICAL HISTORY ON VIC

Having grown up during the war was perfect for playing his spectacular role in *Oh What a Lovely War* which we have deep regrets to say closed

96

up in January of '65. But previous to this as you may know Victor was in Theatre Workshop or as was formerly called the Theatre Royal in the East end of London. *OWALW* opened here March 19th, 1963, and because of its stupendability moved up to Wyndham's Theatre that June. Here it played until about June 27, 1964, a year later.

Anyone who was connected with this show will tell you he is the most loyal person now as he was then. As well as this fine trait, Victor has been known to have an adhesive personality and is a lover of practical jokes.

August 1964 brought the cast to Edinburgh Festival where he played in *Henry IV* parts I and II. But as the saying goes "You can't win them all" and it didn't.

His roles in the theatre have varied from a film cameraman in *Behind the Iron Mask* to Bert Sweetly in a story about an American who had a bad habit of chewing gum. From gum chewer he jumped to a Marquis in *Candide*. Here's a character that ought to turn your mind batty: Eartha, an ugly stepsister in *Cinderella*. He ran around wearing a gold evening gown singing "I'm Going to the Ball." Well it takes all kinds and I guess this is why he is such a fascinating character.

Victor has made several American television appearances. You may have caught him on Johnny Carson's show in January. He did his drill master's skit from *OWALW*. Then again he sat and talked with Jack Paar on January 29. That evening he told a hilarious story about his black-haired mother. Seems she has a knack for "determining" the future. Isn't that right, Victor?

If you were one of the very fortunate people you saw him perform on *That Was the Week That Was*. He sang a refreshing French song, so refreshing that I can't remember the name of it. (Did you notice how glimmering his eyes were? They are always beautiful just like two big jelly beans.)

CONGRATULATIONS

We have in our midst, Victor Spinetti Fan Club members, a very talented young lady named Nancy. She is a high school senior at West Catholic

Girls and brought fame to her school by taking second prize in a poster contest representing Poison Prevention Week. Congratulations Nancy.

If any other of our members would happen to be so talented as to make the newsstands, we would appreciate your sending in your name and address so you too may receive credit where credit is due.

Just write to us.

APRIL 21, 1965

Victor Spinetti our secret agent 008 1/4 has informed his fan club that he will be working on the Beatle movie until the middle of May. Then he goes to New York City to do a guest shot on *The Jack Paar Show*.

APRIL 28, 1965

We heard that the Beatles are coming to America this summer and not appearing in Philadelphia. We are not happy, to say the very least.

Teen to Teen

By Patti & Diane

When the Beatles return to the U.S.A. in the summer months, they will be busy in Hollywood taping two hour-long T.V. specials.

AN OPEN LETTER TO THE BEATLES

We, your loyal fans in Philly are making a final plea. As one of the largest cities in the U.S., many of our girls were unable to obtain tickets as you are so popular. You have made yourself available in Ohio and New York but you have passed us by. Have you forgotten the hundreds of thousands of Beatle recordings we have purchased? Is it that we Philly Birds just don't seem to flip your hair? We are just as loyal as the birds in Mexico City or Miami, if not more so. Was it the reception we gave you last September that wasn't good enough for you? Did we hurt your feelings, decrease your dignity?

We, the teens of Philly, are wishing you would reconsider a return trip to our town. It would give numerous girls that one chance to see you.

Think it over and maybe if you can't decide for yourselves, just ask Victor Spinetti for some sound advice.

MAY 1, 1965

Since we luv just about all British groups, and are one big happy family, we wouldn't have missed the concert featuring some English groups earlier tonight. Here's what happened:

The show at Convention Hall was good. Herman's Hermits stole the hearts of just about everyone. The Stones put on a pretty good act, but they seemed disinterested with the whole bit. Little Anthony and the Imperials were great (as always) and had the whole place jumping. It seems having "Influence" means everything there at Convention Hall. There were the lucky teens who were backstage and made it known to all the "poor" unimportant people in the audience. They sat right on the side of the stage where all could see them. At least they should not have shown themselves onstage. But as you know, these people had "Influence" and could do what they pleased.

MAY 3, 1965

Yesterday when I turned sixteen, I hosted a party in the dining room. Mom and I had an enormous argument about the guest list. It was *my* party and I wanted *my* friends, but she insisted on inviting the old relatives. We set a truce: my friends sat around the table smiling at my eighty-two-year-old Italian grandmother and my Great Aunt Kate. It worked out OK after all. Grandmom enjoyed herself, Aunt Kate told some great stories, and the girls had a fun afternoon, too. Best part of the party: I got to wear my new white Chelsea-look dress.

But I am saving the best for last, as the most exciting part of my Sweet Sixteen birthday was the special gift sent by our Victor. Mom (how can I be annoyed at her?) wrote to Victor on location to ask for Paul's autograph as a birthday surprise. Sent in a Salzburg Hotel Edelweiss envelope, but postmarked from London, was this letter:

```
London: March 30, 1965
Dear Patti
I showed your picture to Paul and told him it
was your birthday—he wrote greetings to you on
the enclosed postcard where we were filming and
I got the studio hairdresser to get me a lock of
his hair. So what more can you want?
    Happy Birthday too
    From Victor
    Will be on the film six weeks more. Buy April
and May Rave, also Seventeen.
```

Enclosed was a shiny black-and-white postcard with six views of the Austrian Alps: skiers, ski lifts, and the Salzburg crest. Written on the back in black ink was the personal greeting from Paul. "To Patti from Paul McCartney Happy Birthday Love!"

My heart skipped a beat, but then . . .

Inside the envelope was the holy grail of Beatles relics, a lock of Paul's hair cut at Twickenham Studio in London where he is filming the movie. It is about three inches long in a "C" shape and is a wonderful color—sort of a rich chestnut brown. I held it up next to my own dark hair, but mine appears nearly black compared to Paul's very rich brown locks. Want to hear a secret? I now sleep each night with Paul's hair, which I encased in clear plastic, under my pillow. Maybe I will dream of him. At least, I have a head start.

How can I ever thank Victor for this gift of all gifts?

MAY 15, 1965

Phyllis Battelle, who is a journalist for Hearst Headline Service, wrote all about our dear Victor in an article called "Victor Is Second Banana to a Bonanza" for her *Assignment: America* column. Victor mentioned his fan clubs: "I got off a bus in Philadelphia recently and there was a crowd of girls, screaming, wondered, 'Who's on this bus?' And then they mobbed me, forced me to eat

Cosy-Verlag, Alfred Gründler, Salzburg, Getreidegasse Nr. 22

To Patti

from

Paul McCartney

Happy Birthday, love !

Echte Photographie

a chocolate cake labeled 'We love you, Victor!' and told me they'd formed a Victor Spinetti fan club. Actually, I represented only tangible evidence that the Beatles really do exist—I was something they had touched in the line of duty—and that's why I now have fan clubs in Chicago, Philadelphia and New York. However, I like to think that as they get to know me, my fan clubs are beginning to rather like me—for myself." The rest of the article is wonderful. It also mentions how Victor recently received the Antoinette Perry Award for starring on Broadway in *Oh What a Lovely War.*

MAY 20, 1965

Diane decided to go to the airport in style to meet the *Shindig!* road show. Her idea: decorate her dad's car—and I do mean decorate. She taped dozens of Beatles photos inside the car along with balloons and streamers. Then she added some exterior touches. We rode to the airport in style to wait with other fans to catch a glimpse of the groups as they arrived. No one arrived in a car quite like Diane's Beatle-mobile.

MAY 21, 1965

Then tonight, *Shindig!* came to Philly. No, not on the boob tube, but in honest-to-gosh person. The stars that came with it were Gerry and the Pacemakers, Shirley Ellis, the Dixie Cups, Joey Page, and Roosevelt Greer. Some of the *Shindig!* dancers came along too and did their stuff. All in all, it was a pretty delightful evening, for the auditorium was small, and unlike in Convention Hall, you had a good view of everything. We have to admit, though, that Gerry and his lads got the whole place jumping. Let's hope they return to Philly soon.

One thing, though. Gerry's drummer had a girl perched on his lap throughout the concert. Somehow, it just didn't seem right. I had never seen that before. He must have really liked her.

Tickets were four dollars each at the Hotel Philadelphia Ballroom, Broad and Vine Streets, in the heart of town.

MAY 25, 1965

A certain nosy person has stuck her head in these pages. Some people have to spoil all the fun of writing in a secret diary. I don't care who it is, they have *no* right to my private property.

School will be out in a few weeks. I miss Victor very much. I'll never see him again, most likely, because I am not allowed to New York City again. Can't wait till I'm thirty-nine, then I'll be "allowed" to go.

Jamie is still foremost in my mind, but what's the use of dreaming?

MAY 26, 1965

In *Teen to Teen* today—008 1/4 is about to return. Yes, after all those months filming the Beatles' second movie (which is either entitled *Eight Arms to Hold You* or *Help!*), good old Victor Spinetti is arriving in New York City on Wednesday. Let's have a bigggg welcome back from all of us. And for all of us fans who are wondering why the Beatles passed our fair city by on their next tour, we have the scoop in our column! Vic has stated they have nothing whatsoever to do with their tour plans. It's not them who name the towns they perform in.

Heard on the radio—and sung by us fans . . .

```
We luv you Ring-GO
Oh yes we dooo
We luv you Rin-GO
And we'll be trueee
When you're not near to us
We're BLUE
Oh, Rin-GO
We luv yooou
Yeah-Yeah-Yeah-Ye-ah
```

(In the following three choruses, substitute "John," "Paul," and "George.")

JUNE 10, 1965

It's all over. I heard a rumor over the radio that my Jamie is now engaged. My little world went KER-PLUNK! I really miss him, and my heart really hurts. It will only be a matter of time till James Paul McCartney makes Jane Asher his bride. I am trying to forget him, for I don't want my heart to feel this way anymore. It's been a fun year and a half. Jamie has made me grow up in a lot of ways, and maybe it's time for him to leave off, for his job is finished. Maybe someone else will pick up where my dear Jamie left off. I will always think of this era of my life that has just come to an end.

Never will I forget my Jamie!

To mark this very sad occasion, I had a good cry—and then left wet tear splotches on the wallpaper in my room. Underneath, in pencil, I printed so you could hardly see it: "PAUL ENGAGED."

JUNE 18, 1965

Ah, how can I leave this crazy part of my life? Happy birthday, Paul! Wish I could be with you to help celebrate with a cake and then maybe a night out on the town in London. I wish. I wish.

JUNE 19, 1965

Diane and I did it. We borrowed two press passes and got into the Dave Clark Five press conference today. Had great seats—smack dab in the front row. Some other young "journalists" tried to push us out of the seats, but we held fast. We had a fab view of the Five. I was lookin' good in my white eyelet dress with my new white stockings. Later we hung around the Warwick Hotel to meet the group, but only got as far as the bathroom on the first floor . . .

Sadly, the day wasn't perfect. Some idiot stole my "I Love Paul" Beatle button off of my cute purse. It was one of the first Beatle things I ever bought, and you can't buy them anymore. I will miss it and hope the thief gets her finger cut on the pin.

Our column on the DC5 will appear on Wednesday.

JUNE 23, 1965

Teen to Teen

By Patti & Diane

SPECIAL! Your lucky columnists were fortunate enough to obtain two front row seats to the Dave Clark Five private press conference held at the Warwick Hotel on Saturday, June nineteenth. The conference, originally scheduled for five in the afternoon, didn't actually take place until 6:30. It seems the traffic coming from New York tied the group up quite badly. They were in New York for an Ed Sullivan taping. When the Five finally marched in with their police escort, the fun really began. The questions, mainly pointed at Dave and Mike, went something like this: What do you think of being back in Philly, Dave? "Well, it's great to be back here." Someone at this point spoke up and stated that Dave looked like Hercules, whereupon Dave answered, "My dog is called Hercules." They informed the press that their next tour will be after January, and when asked how they got into the recording business, Rick jokingly answered "Through a door." When asked about their favorite American group they all answered in unison "The Supremes!" Dave said that the Byrds, Bob Dylan and Beach Boys were also quite popular in English circles. While sipping tea it was asked of Mike, what did he think of the American type of tea? He explained, "It's diabolical—just like English coffee!" A brave soul supplied Mike with this question, how did he like to see girls dressed? His witty answer was "In clothes." He added though that girls should dress smartly and with style. Lenny congratulated the Beatles on winning the English Medal of Honor while Dave stated, "The medal is for those in the entertainment field as well as the battle field." At about 7:00 P.M. this most interesting conference came to an end, and as Denny winked at us our day seemed complete.

JUNE 25, 1965

Only six more months till Christmas! Somehow I am so very, very bored. Bored to tears. I have been helping around the house, but that's about all. I don't understand life—something always switches the hopeless to the hopeful, and vice versa. Right now I can think of at least three situations I would like to change. Oh, I am so mixed up. Please someone find something to get me out of this boredom.

JULY 10, 1965

I just heard that the new *Beatles VI* album went to number one in the country! It is now sitting in my album rack under my stereo set. I own quite a collection of Beatles LPs. Think if I had a bratty little sister to mess up my record collection. Not fun at all. The cover of *Beatles VI* is gear: all four Lads are smiling in full color! Paul and George wear dark, skinny ties and long-sleeved dress shirts, while John is tieless. Poor Ringo is in the background in a classic dark turtleneck. I feel sad for him there, way in the back. *Beatles VI* includes the remaining songs left off *Beatles '65*. Lots of great songs here, but my favorites are "Eight Days a Week," Buddy Holly's "Words of Love," "Dizzy Miss Lizzy," and "Kansas City/Hey, Hey, Hey, Hey." "What You're Doing" is a fun song, too.

JULY 13, 1965

Here are some of the articles I have been reading in the June and July issues of 16 *Magazine*. "The Secret Confession of George Harrison." "What It Is Like to Be Married to Ringo!" "Pattie Boyd's Letter from London" where hemlines are still rising and are now about one inch above the knee. "The Rolling Stones as We Know Them," by their mums.

I keep my magazines in a huge stack near my bed. Mom is always begging me to throw them out, but I say, "Never."

JULY 15, 1965

Got a letter today from Victor, which was posted from Riverhead, New York. He wrote to us about the major newspaper articles we have sent him that mentioned his fan clubs. We were upset that they got the info all wrong, but Victor "cleared the air."

Dear All in Philly

Hope this letter wasn't too much but we must clear the air. The article in today's *New York Sunday Times* is a perfect example. I told the interviewer that *you* had the sweater and *you* were the first but he got it wrong. But what the hell—they got the name right and it is a New York paper. So don't get upset down there . . .

It is impossible to have complete *control* over what they say in the papers, for instance in London they've printed that I despise England. I didn't say that but they published it. Now let's all be friends again. Please remember I am very fond of you all. I have *no* control over what is published—I'm lucky to have so many things printed. Look at the best side always. Be happy that we are friends. Stop complaining about *your-selves.* Think what you can do for others. Stop complaining about me. I love you all but stop putting me on trial all the time.

Love

Victor

JULY 23, 1965

Time to straighten out my Beatles stuff. My collection is growing—posters, buttons, records, books, magazines, bubblegum cards, a charm bracelet with tiny Beatle faces, and even a scarf! Mom keeps asking me to put it all together in a closet. Before she reaches the volcano stage, I guess I should tidy it all up.

Going through my Beatle bubblegum collection, I discovered that I own four different series for a grand total of 101 cards. That is a lot of bubblegum and, hopefully, no trips to the dentist to repair cavities. I mostly have the first (nos. 1 through 60), second (nos. 61 through 115), and third series of cards (nos. 116 through 165). The black-and-white photos show individual close-ups of the Liverpool Lads as well as candids, stage, tour, and publicity shots. One (no. 102) of the Beatles is a hoot, as their faces are superimposed with crew cuts! Someone had a real sense of humor. Only the numbers and series are marked on the back, and no text. Darn it. The third series is more of the same. I forgot to mention that each card has a Beatle signature in blue.

The fourth group of black-and-white cards is from the Beatles movie *A Hard Day's Night* series. These photos were taken on the set. Best of all, they are numbered on the back with two or three sentences as captions. Number 17 shows Ringo and a young boy from a scene in the film.

The fifth group I own is BEATLES COLOR CARDS. These cards are gear. Many of the ones I have in my collection look like they were taken in New York when the Beatles first appeared on *The Ed Sullivan Show*. Some are stage shots, and others are more candid outdoor photos. They are numbered on the back with questions and answers. This series is fun to read and collect.

You can imagine how grateful I was when Sister returned my Beatle bubblegum cards to me after she caught me passing them around during class. I thought it was the end.

AUGUST 4, 1965

Mod styles from London. That is what Diane and I wrote about in our *Teen to Teen* column today. If you dress British, you feel more a part of the "Youthquake Mary Quant" mod scene in London. But not a great deal of mod clothing is worn by the teens hanging on the corners in our neighborhood. Still, we interviewed this gear British fashion designer. It should give our readers an idea on international fashion.

This past Saturday, we had the pleasure of having an interview with the English mod designer Roger Nelson. Mr. Nelson introduced his line of winter styles at Strawbridge and Clothier with a swinging fashion show. Mr. Nelson is a very handsome man with a Beatle cut and a dapper mod suit. He began his career five years ago at Homesey College of Art. He first was an artist but went into designing very shortly after. His designs are very popular in England with the young fashionites known as the mods. He also has designed fashions for girl pop singers such as Marianne Faithfull and Sandy Shaw. Roger's creations last for a season, then he bounces right back with a new line of clothes. America isn't the only place where his chic girl mod styles are catching on. Sweden, France, Ireland, and Bermuda are a few other countries. Roger Nelson was born in Isslington, England, and has come a long way since he lived in that Cockney town.

AUGUST 11, 1965

Help! was definitely the high point of my summer. The newspapers and pop radio stations had us waiting on the edge of our chairs for the premiere. Even the ads in the paper were cute: "Stop worrying! Help is on the way. The Colorful Adventures of THE BEATLES are more Colorful than ever . . . in COLOR! NOW! GIVE MOM AND DAD THE *Help!* THEY NEED! Take them to see *Help* and they'll see what great entertainment really is and how funny the Beatles can be." The movie premiered in five hundred movie houses all around the United States.

We all went by bus to the 69th Street Tower Theater in Upper Darby for the premiere. Lines of Beatles fans stretched around the block for the afternoon matinee. This gave us officers of the O.V.S.F.C.A. an idea. Diane volunteered to wear Victor's fuzzy sweater from *A Hard Day's Night* in the 90 degree heat. Showing off the sweater and its history, we hawked small pieces of sweater fuzz taped on cards with fan club information. We also stuck fan club flyers on cars and managed to duck the cops. It was our best marketing effort of the year. These Beatle fans = fan club members.

When Victor came on-screen, we clapped like mad to show our love and support. My most beloved scene: Paul in his camel-colored suit and soft turtleneck sweater singing "The Night Before" on Salisbury Plain with the wind whipping through his dark hair. I was absolutely paralyzed through that entire song.

When, sadly, it was over, we walked to the Western Union office at 69th Street to send a congratulations telegram to Victor. Unfortunately, we didn't have much money between us after paying for movie tickets, bus fare, and popcorn, so we managed to s-t-r-e-t-c-h the one word we could afford to send him back in London.

We came up with the biggest, most exhilarating word we could spell, and that was "Supercalifragilisticexpialidocious" from Walt Disney's film *Mary Poppins*.

I am sure Victor will know exactly what we mean.

AUGUST 15, 1965

This is what Victor said about filming with the Beatles: "Ouch! My eyes are sore and my ears are burning—and this all comes from too many fab funny moments filming with the Beatles in *Help!* Can the Beatles act? That's what everyone wants to know. I asked John and he said, 'We don't know anything about acting. We just walk round and have our pictures taken!' But he followed that with one of my favorite Beatle lines when he said, 'Why is it that whenever the director shouts action, everyone becomes people, but they aren't?' The Beatles don't—that's their secret, and I felt immensely proud when John said to me, 'But you don't change Victor. Does that mean you are as terrible as we are?'"

AUGUST 20, 1965

Summer is flying by way too fast to suit me. Still, the Beatle Buddies have continued this season of *Help!* After seeing the film once, twice, three times, we all went out to buy the album. Listening to *Help!* brought back all the great moments from the movie. As of today, I luv all the songs but can do without the sound track instrumentals. There is so much to enjoy: "Help!," "The Night Before," "You've Got to Hide Your Love Away," "I Need

You," "Another Girl," "Ticket to Ride," and "You're Going to Lose That Girl." The Beatles are spelling out something in code with their outstretched arms on the album cover. They are dressed like snow bunnies for the Austrian Alps. This one is an unusual album cover.

AUGUST 24, 1965

We seem to make the daily papers a lot these days. Since we have been marketing the fan club in a big way, Diane sent a membership to one of the *Philadelphia Bulletin*'s top columnists. Mr. Smart contacted Diane, and the column appeared today in the daily paper.

AUGUST 25, 1965

Didn't get the chance to see the Beatles perform at Shea Stadium in New York on August 15, but wrote a special report about the concert in our *Teen to Teen* column today.

Dressed in black pants, khaki-colored jackets, "They" sang twelve songs, which lasted about forty minutes. They started off with "Twist and Shout" and ended with the ear-splitting "I'M DOWN," with John playing the organ with his feet instead of his fingers. Paul looked rather exhausted, as did the others. Even though it was the first concert of the tour, George's hair was about the longest and all the mops had turned a lighter hue it seemed. Ringo wasn't quite himself—singing only one song and not shaking his head. And, of course, John and Paul acted naturally, with their usual bouncy ways.

In Our Town

They Own Spinetti Fuzz, Beatle Hair

By James Smart

A LETTER ARRIVED the other day which informed me that as of Aug. 19 I had become an honorary member of the Victor Spinetti Fan Club of America, Original Chapter No. 1, Philadelphia.

That's almost as good as being made an honorary teenager.

Being one of those rare and courageous adults who will admit that he likes the Beatles, I happened to know who Victor Spinetti is.

He has played in both Beatle movies. In the first one he was the television director with the fuzzy sweater. In the current one, "Help!," he is a mad scientist.

I called Diane Lamont, president of the Original Chapter No. 1, to thank her for my official membership card and to ask how come the Original Chapter of the VSFC of A. was formed in Southwest Philadelphia.

"WE'RE BEATLES ALL the way," she told me. "That's how we met Victor. His picture was in the papers last September when he was playing in, 'Oh, What a Lovely War.' We recognized him and stayed outside the stage door until we met him."

Diane and her friends started the club on Sept. 29, and have been in touch with Spinetti ever since. Some of them had lunch with him in New York last week, where he is studying his role in a new play, "The Skyscraper," with Julie Harris.

"He sends us things, too," said Diane, "like the fuzzy sweater he wore in the movie, swizzle sticks the Beatles used, and some of their cigaret butts, and Paul McCartney's hair . . ."

Victor Spinetti

"Where did he get the hair?" I asked.

"At Twickenham Studios," she said. "The Beatles got their hair cut on the set. It was Pat's birthday (Patricia Gallo, co-president of the Original Chapter) so Victor sent it to her and Paul wrote 'happy birthday.'"

"Where do you keep all the club's relics?" I asked.

"I have the sweater hanging on a hook in my room," she said. "We give fuzz from it to all the members. We have about 100 members. There are other chapters all over, I keep everything except the hair and the candles from George's birthday cake . . ."

"What candles?"

"Victor sent candles from George's birthday cake from the Bahamas for my girl friend Joanne Burns, secretary of the club."

"And I didn't even get any fuzz from Victor Spinetti's sweater," I said.

"I'll send you some fuzz," said Diane, "if you really want."

Reproduced with permission from the Special Collections Research Center, Temple University Libraries, Philadelphia, PA.

Even though they didn't get to Philly, the Beatles are playing nine cities on the tour and will fly home on September 1. Too bad they didn't make it here. The Lads missed the very best city in America!

AUGUST 27, 1965
Paging through my Beatles Scrapbooks Volumes I and II, I spotted some gear poetry my friends and I scribbled to decorate the pages:

```
They hold the world,
But not as the world,
A stage—
Where each Beatle
Must play his part.
*
Fans Know:
Every Paul must have his Jane,
But somehow we don't seem the same.
*
Philly Falls in Frightful Frenzy (Fab)
*
They came,
They saw,
They conquered hearts.
Somehow they left
of them—a part.
*
To these girls
Who stand on chairs,
I'd like to take,
And box their ears.
(Dumb girls at concerts)
*
```

Leave us sad—
Or leave us harried,
But please please DON'T
Leave us married.
*
Ringo, Ringo
Tonsils out,
Now maybe—
We'll hear you
Twist and Shout!
*
Paul McCartney—
Are you married?
Are you not?
Rumors fly
Like birds in the sky.
*
Ringo Starr—
Although married you are,
Some fans—
Still worship you from afar.
*
2 Down
2 To Go
= 4 Beatles
*
Ringo—
It was only yesterday you said
You wouldn't get hitched
Unless you were dead.

SEPTEMBER 1, 1965

Funny how all the experts go on and on about what the Beatles are doing to today's young people. One article, "Is Beatlemania a Passing Fad?" by Joseph Whitney (King Features Syndicate, 1964), quoted a British physician, Dr. F. R. C. Casson. He said, "Rhythmic sound has a strong effect on the human brain. The frenzied dancing of Voodoo worshippers, the howls and writhing of converts among primitive evangelical sects, and the screams of Beatle fans, are just different ways of letting off emotional steam. This is a source of much relief and pleasure; more so when the excitement has been built up and maintained at a high level."

Huh?

Yet another insight into our Beatlemaniac brains from child psychiatrist Dr. Robert C. Prall:

A Child Psychiatrist Looks at the

By DR. ROBERT C. PRALL

As told to
FRED R. ZEPP

AS A PRACTICING child psychiatrist, I have some simple advice for craze-harried parents of teen-agers: Don't let the Beatles bug you.

They're just a fad. And the fad will fade.

True, whatever replaces the mop-headed yeah-yeah-yeah quartet is sure to be just as hard on adult nerves. Maybe even worse. But the point is, don't get too worked up over the Beatles or whoever else may be the idol of the malt-shop set for the moment. It's all a perfectly normal part of growing up.

I see it in my own family. I have three children in their teens: Patricia, 19, a student at Miami University in Oxford, Ohio, now on a leave of absence to serve as an assistant teacher; Louise, 18, who is studying at Duke University to become a nurse, and John, 16, a pupil at Harriton High School in Lower Merion Township.

Between my children, their friends, and the dozens I come in contact with daily in my work, there hasn't been a teen-age craze in the last couple of decades that hasn't made itself noisily in my eardrums.

Almost all these crazes share the same basic causes. The Beatles are no exception.

They've swept the teen-agers of the Western world, largely because of the kids' need to belong.

In the 12- to 14-year-old crowd especially, but lapping over a couple of years to include 16s and even 18s in some cases, one of the paramount objects in life is to be accepted—to be "in," "hep," "with it." Conversely, the worst thing that can happen is to be an outsider—"a square."

Most parents know this. They see it when their boys and girls insist on doing what the others do —wearing the same hair-do, the same shoes, the same tight pants, the same sweaters. Actually, this is part of growing up, of learning to conform to society.

One of the things a teen-ager must do to be "in" is listen to the crowd's favorite radio station—and every area has at least one, geared to the teens' interest level. It's practically mandatory to like the same music as everyone else, so if one of these stations—or, more likely, several of them—swing a sizable group of teen-agers behind some star or musical group, the enthusiasm surges upward like a missile.

That's a good part of the Beatles' foundation.

For through these radio stations, it has become "in" to enjoy the Beatles. The next step has been to buy their records; as boys and girls visit in each other's homes, and are

increasingly exposed to more and more Beatles records, the craze mushrooms.

Of course, there has to be more to it than conformity, although that's the biggest item.

There's sex, for one thing.

Medically speaking, there is absolutely nothing physiological about all this fainting and swooning which seems to sweep young female Beatle addicts.

On the other hand, this is the age at which interest in the opposite sex is starting up. Anything which stimulates this interest— such as Elvis Presley's pelvis-wiggling or the Beatles' swaying—catches their eyes fast.

When you couple that with the mop-tops' thumping, primitive rhythm and chants of yeah, yeah, yeah, you have a combination which helps induce the girls to squeal.

HOWEVER, parents will remember how teen-agers of long ago squealed for Frank Sinatra. Before that, for Rudy Vallee. Some girl, sometime, squealed and the idea stuck: it became, again, the thing to do. It's a combination of some sex appeal, plus being "in."

The boys don't do this when they hear the Beatles; for most of them, voices are changing. Aside from feeling awkward, they fear to

scream because their voices might (horror of horrors) crack in public.

But girls are more effervescent than boys, anyway. They get a real charge out of being able to cry out, "I touched a Beatle!" Or, "I saw one!" They're the ones who make the noise, just as they were the ones who stormed the gates at Convention Hall to buy Beatles tickets in advance.

Then, next, comes the element of rebellion.

At this age, children stage a revolt against adult standards. Anything grownups like is bad; whatever grownups are against is good. From the start, most parents apparently have been against the Beatles. Therefore, in their offspring's eyes, the Beatles have to be marvelous.

This ties in with the Beatles' haircuts, if that's the right description. All through their lives, most teen-age boys have been made to keep their hair neat; this is a parental command. As a result, the boys want it long and shaggy. The Beatles come along and show off an enviable wild mop of hair. Bingo! That's the hairdo to have. The more the old folks object, the more desirable it becomes.

If parents wanted dirty, uncombed, flowing locks on their sons, chances are the boys w...

SEPTEMBER 6, 1965

The September issue of 16 *Magazine* featured "Kiss Your Favorite Beatle," with life-sized lips of each one plus cute portraits on the right. I immediately cut them out and stuck them up on my bedroom wall. There they joined my six-foot-tall poster of Paul, an assortment of Beatles posters—and a gear smiling full-color head shot of guess who? That delightful photo is taped on my ceiling directly over my pillow. Sweet dreams, oh yeah.

Still, my room doesn't come close to Diane's bedroom, which is plastered with Beatles up, down, over, and under. We even ran a snapshot of her Beatles room with our *Teen to Teen* column.

Diane is so lucky. She is the only one of us to have her very own *Help!* box in her room. I think she said it was from Jolly's Record Store on Woodland Avenue. Part of the promotion for the movie LP, the box, which plugs into the wall, is so cool. When the lid opens, a cartoon hand wearing a ring pops up. The *Help!* box is one great souvenir. I bet not many fans have such a trophy in their own rooms.

SEPTEMBER 7, 1965

Yes, I do have Beatles posters on my bedroom walls, but I am really proud of my metal book shelf that Dad assembled for me. It is nothing fancy, but it helps to hold my library of Beatles information. My fave books from grammar school are here: *Jane Eyre, National Velvet,* and *Ben Hur.*

My Beatles library includes *In His Own Write* by John Lennon, *A Cellarful of Noise* by Brian Epstein, *The Beatles in "Help!": A Novel* by Al Hine, *The Beatles in "A Hard Day's Night"* by John Burke, and my Beatles Scrapbooks Volumes I and II. I also own a bunch of Beatles magazines, which I now stack on my shelf and not on the floor. Keeping things neat makes for a happy mom. Meanwhile, my collection grows and grows.

SEPTEMBER 14, 1965

Back to school again! This is junior year, and I am not too thrilled about wearing those dingy green jumpers with the dull beige blouses. It was fun to see my friends again on the first day of school, but I am sure I am heading into a difficult study year. I am taking chemistry, Italian, French, history, religion, and English and hope to join the *Reaper,* which is the school newspaper. I don't think I will have trouble with the nuns and teachers, as I am rather quiet. Sure hope it will go well. The Beatle Buddies celebrated the beginning of the brand-new school year with a VIP (Very Important Program).

THE DAY WE SACRIFICED JANE ASHER: Taking a page out of *Help!* where Ringo finds himself the human sacrifice target of a cult, we decided to sacrifice Paul's girlfriend Jane Asher at sixth-period lunch. Diane creatively constructed a clay voodoo doll with corncob holder arms. The idea was to stick some safety pins in the Asher-Smasher doll during lunch and check the papers later to see if Paul broke up with her. Poor Barbara didn't make it to the Lunch Sacrifice Ceremony—which echoed a scene in *Help!* where the guy on crutches states, "I'm going to miss the sacrifice." We were lucky that the nun patrolling the lunchroom didn't catch us in the act.

It was a great way to start the school year.

SEPTEMBER 17, 1965

Did I mention about our guitar lessons? Both Jean and I started lessons a while back. We bought cheap guitars, and I changed my strings around because I am left-handed just like Paul. I had to cart the guitar on the trolley into Center City Philly once a week to my lesson. After a few lessons, I discovered I should stick to writing. Now, Jean, on the other hand, is a natural and plays the guitar beautifully—just like her George.

This week after school we were all in town and Jean was carting her guitar case with her before a lesson. Hungry, we stopped at a small corner Italian restaurant for an early dinner. Suddenly, we all thought of the scene in the movie *Ferry Cross the Mersey* starring the Liverpool group Gerry and the Pacemakers.

In the film, the group starts singing and playing the guitar in a restaurant and didn't have to pay the check. So Jean started strumming her guitar, but the check came anyway. We pooled our allowances and thankfully had enough cash to settle the bill.

That was the end of *Ferry Cross the Mersey* and our "free" dinner.

SEPTEMBER 19, 1965

Since I was born with two left feet, dancing was never my strongpoint. While other little neighborhood girls were bundled off to Miss Betty's dance class, I opted for hiking in Fairmount Park with the Brownie Scouts. Nor do I have the gumption to spring across the street from our high school after classes to dance on *Bandstand*.

At Kathy's insistence, I was taken against my better judgment to Chez-Vous Ballroom. We met the other girls at the bus stop and wore our comfortable shoes for dancing. Walking from the bus to the dance was a challenge. Guys cruising around in cars shouted out the windows, "Hey baby—why don't cha go with us?" or the less complimentary "Your hair came outta bottle."

Chez-Vous, which is a combination skating rink and dance arena, features a teen hop every Friday night hosted by Deejay Jerry Blavat aka the Geator with the Heater or the Boss with the Hot Sauce. We kids line up in front of the building at 7050 Terminal Square in Upper Darby, pay our dollar admission, and climb the steep flight of stairs. Pop music blares from loud speakers; the vast dance floor is hardwood, and the pillars are the only things that are stationary.

The ballroom has an imaginary dividing line drawn across it. One side is for "Jives" and the other for "Conservatives." Jives are those who are decked out in black leather jackets and tight pants, while their girlfriends are fond of teased bouffant hairdos. Conservatives pride themselves in their Ivy League fashions. The girls style their hair in simple flips and wear A-line skirts and loafers. Both groups have their own way of dancing, talking, and walking. A Jive stepping across the line to dance with a Conservative is akin to Romeo meeting Juliet.

Kathy is Jive. I am mod/Conservative. The tantalizing aroma of sizzling hotdogs was beckoning me from the forbidden zone.

I went over to the other side.

AUTUMN-WINTER 1965-1966

SEPTEMBER 22, 1965

This week in our *Teen to Teen* column, we wished Victor *and* Ringo good luck.

> All the members of the Official Victor Spinetti Fan Club of America would like to take this opportunity to wish Victor all the best in his new Broadway show *Skyscraper,* which is now at tryouts in Detroit. . . .
>
> All our congratulations go to Ringo and Maureen on the birth of their first child on September 13. At last word, the baby and Mo and Ringo were just fine, and they decided to name the bouncing boy Zak. Ringo says it is a bit biblical, but a little Western too.

OCTOBER 2, 1965

Thought about what really makes a Beatles fan a Beatles fan. It seems we can always spot others in a crowd or at school. It certainly isn't only the music but so many more pieces of the puzzle that make us "*the* fans." Some of the items on this list may have been more popular last year during the initial frenzy, for example, the short "Beatle" cut, but these are only my ideas. While it is true that most of us are teenage girls, there are boy fans, granny fans, and who-knows-who-else fans.

The Making of a Beatlemaniac
- Beatle buttons pinned on purse or clothes
- "John Lennon" cap
- Long, straight hair with "Beatle bangs"
- Or short "Beatle cut" with "Beatle bangs"
- Mod fashions from London
- Beatle jewelry: ID or charm bracelets and pins
- Mimicking Liverpool slang and British accent
- Room and/or car decorated in "early Beatles"
- Entering Beatles contests and writing soulful poetry
- Defending the Liverpool Lads to the press
- Hanging out wherever a British rock group may appear
- Watching Beatles films several times and memo- rizing dialogue
- Collecting Beatles stuff: albums, magazines, dolls, etc.
- Adoring one special Beatle as your very own
- And above all . . . loyalty to the cause
Oh, and so much more.

OCTOBER 9, 1965
Happy twenty-fifth birthday to John! Conveniently, his birthday was on a Saturday this year, and what better way to celebrate the occasion than with a party at my house? Found a genuine Beatles birthday cake with a

sugary medallion of the "Four Moptops" in the center. Looked too good to eat, but we managed. I decorated the table with a copy of Lennon's book *In His Own Write*. At each setting, I set a handwritten place card featuring the Beatle of choice, for example, "Patti Gallo aka Mrs. Paul McCartney." Once again, I tacked my Beatles posters up on the wall of the dining room.

Didn't attempt to call Liverpool or London this time, but Kathy and the Beatle Buddies did agree it was a good party. Too bad John couldn't make it.

OCTOBER 15, 1965

Had yet another argument with my mom! She, for some reason unknown to me, won't let me take the train to New York with the girls to see Victor on Broadway. He is in rehearsal for *Skyscraper,* a new play on Broadway. How I wish I was old enough to be out on my own.

NOVEMBER 7, 1965

It was bound to happen and it did. Last night, I went on my very first date—a blind date actually—and no, it was not with darling Paul. Oh, how I wish it had been him who sat across from me during dinner. Let me write this down as fast as I can. The niece of my mom's best friend lives in South Philly and is a high school senior. She is sweet and has a boyfriend who has a friend . . . well, you get the idea. We double dated last night at the Harvey House Restaurant in town on Broad Street. This was the very same place we shared ice cream with Victor.

Who teaches you what to do or how to act on a first date? I was not sure what to wear or where to put my hands or who opens the door or where to sit or even who grabs the check at the end of the meal. On top of that, everyone ordered chicken in a basket. I absolutely hate to eat any food that comes in a plastic basket, not to mention tackling finger food at a restaurant in front of the whole world. Well, I did get through the evening, although it was definitely not my idea of a night to remember.

The date was a nice guy, really, but not my type. I like them tall, dark, and handsome—and that, my friend, is a curse for plain girls such as yours truly.

DECEMBER 22, 1965

Guess what I just heard on the radio? The Beatles' annual Christmas message. Well, actually, just part of it, but John, Paul, George, and Ringo managed to talk nonsense, ad lib their songs, and thank the fans for a fab year. One cute bit:

```
Yesterday, doo-dah,
All my troubles seemed so far away,
Now it looks as though they're here to stay,
Oh, I believe in Christmas Day.
(Bless you all on Christmas Day.)
```

DECEMBER 24, 1965

This Christmas Eve was certainly a washout for Diane and me. This is the very sad tale of what happened to us earlier today:

We heard that Wilfrid Brambell, the actor who portrayed Paul's grandfather in *A Hard Day's Night,* is appearing right now in a play at Philadelphia's Shubert Theater. The two of us stood shivering in the winter rain for six hours today on Christmas Eve waiting outside the theater until rehearsals were over. Unfortunately, Mr. Brambell is not Victor Spinetti and ignored us completely. I guess he is tired of Beatles fans flocking around him. Anyhow, to hide our sorrow, Diane and I sang Christmas carols on the trolley ride home.

I am just now drying out. Merry Christmas to all, except Wilfrid Brambell.

Sometimes I wonder what I am doing, and why. Got to run to get ready for midnight Mass.

JANUARY 5, 1966

Made the daily papers again. Can you believe it? Jack Helsel, editor of the *Teen Scene* column for the *Philadelphia Daily News,* interviewed me and included a head shot. Not the best picture, as my chin looked seven feet long, but still, I was honored.

JANUARY 21, 1966

Here we go again! George married cute blonde model Pattie Boyd earlier today at the Registry Office in Epsom, Surrey, England. Paul and manager Brian Epstein were best men. Poor Jean didn't speak to us the whole day at school. We tried to comfort her because we do understand. Three Beatles are now married men. It is so hard when a Beatle gets married and leaves diehard fans in shock. I mean, so many of us haven't even had a real first date yet.

Maybe we are beginning to feel our age a bit. We are high school juniors, after all, and not freshmen anymore. I still can see Jean's sad face in my mind tonight. How will she cope this weekend without us hovering around?

FEBRUARY 2, 1966

I thought you might like to see what we are up to these days with the *Teen to Teen* column. Not only does all the gossip we can find appear in ink but so do local teen news and popular "teen messages" from readers.

Teen to Teen

By Patti

Ringo told a reporter shortly before the Lennon–McCartney T.V. Special in Manchester that he was perturbed by the knocking articles on the Beatles recently. He said, "I'll have to do something heroic for the sake of publicity. Perhaps I can swim across the MERSEY RIVER in a polyethylene bag with a pile of our L.P.'s on my head." Then a reporter asked him if he wanted son Zak to be a Beatle just like him to which he replied, "Don't be daft!"

***

Keith Richards has a habit of putting things like pencil or paper in his mouth while he's thinking. Aboard a London bus some weeks ago, Keith rolled up his bus ticket and stuck it in his mouth. Their road manager leaned over and Keith absentmindedly took a light from him. You should have seen his face when what he thought was a cigarette, shriveled up and almost set fire to his eyebrows.

***

Although he would be the last person to admit it, Mick Jagger is a very understanding and patient person. If he believes a friend to be miserable, he'll spend hours sitting and talking out their problems with them.

***

Congrats go out to Mr. Jack Helsel who writes the switched on column "Teen Scene" in the *Daily News*. He is the new talent-finder on the Aquarama Dance Show on Saturday afternoon on Channel 3. Tune in to see this great guy who helps teens get a start in show biz.

***

One of the most amusing sights of last year was Herman dancing with LuLu in the Manchester Photographic Club on the occasion of her 17th birthday—in football boots. Studs and all.

***

THE SLIGHTLY SICK DEPARTMENT: Paul McCartney piled three little piles of cigarette ash on the dressing room table and inquired—"Have you heard this one?" Paul addressed the heaps of ash severely, "Will the real Joan of Arc stand up please?"

***

FACTS ABOUT THE BYRDS: Mike Clarke sometimes wears a blue hairnet over his blonde hair, he is a taller version of Brian Jones, won't get out of bed, a fantastic hair washer. Dave Crosby: Suede cap wearer—won't let it out of his sight—wears it in 103 degrees of L.A. sunshine. Chris Hillman: Cutting humor when he wants, quietly cool, walks in a room without being noticed. Gene Clark: Likes the word "Groovy," writes a lot for the group, easy going. Jim McGuinn: Really needs his glasses, exchanges letters and discs with George Harrison.

***

Bob Dylan is a folk singer who has broken all rules—and won. He speaks the "truth" and for this reason several T.V. networks, who have booked him for shows, told him he would have to cut out some of his outspoken lyrics. He refused and never appeared on the shows.

***

TEEN MESSAGES

Skip—
I'll always love you.
Linda

Mike—
Betsy is the only girl for you.

Joey N.—
Theresa B. likes you a lot.
O.W.R.K.

Jimmy R.—
Arlene likes Frankie S.
"70"

FEBRUARY 9, 1966

Cold, dark, and miserable. This time of year drives me nuts. Every school morning is the same: dress in that drab green uniform, grab breakfast on the run, and shiver in the cold waiting for the trolley on Elmwood Avenue. Then it's another wait underground in the dank 30th Street Station to switch to the shiny silver El train to 46th and Market. Don't forget the long day in bor-ing classes with nuns who drone on and on and on.

What's a high school junior to do?

I sing. If I find an unpopulated corner on the El early in the morning, I belt out a tune. The ride is so noisy, so I can sing my heart out. I choose my favorite hits, but at the moment I am bursting out in song with "Downtown" by Petula Clark. It really is so appropriate since I am heading "downtown" in Philadelphia, but not for "movie shows" or "some little places to go to where they never close." Singing—not going downtown—helps to "forget all your troubles, forget all your cares."

It is a great way to start off yet another cold, dark, and miserable day wearing an itchy uniform under a bulky brown corduroy coat on a smelly El train.

FEBRUARY 20, 1966

Kathy, her younger sister, and I started hanging around with the grandson of my dad's godmother. His buddies are so funny, and we have a great time together doing simple things. Some weekends they come over to my place wearing their black leather jackets; other times we go to the movies or just take walks. Only thing is all the guys smoke and we don't. The smell of cigarettes makes me choke. They think they look cool. I will smile through the smoke and ignore it. Is this the penalty you must pay to have guy friends?

MARCH 6, 1966

Jamie (Paul) is still around! But I don't build my life on him anymore. I've learned not to hope for things out of reach. Life is that way. Soon it will be spring and the weather will again be nice. What a long winter it has been! Boys come and go, but the ones I really think are nice never even look my way. So, these are the mysteries of life.

School drags on like an ancient turtle. I look forward to vacation, for I'll be working and earning money like a member of society. I am nearly seventeen years old now. I still have long black hair, but most pimples are gone, braces on my teeth have vanished also, and instead of glasses, I have contact lenses. I am rather slim and small, being five foot three and a half and weighing 106 pounds. I am small boned though.

I feel so old suddenly as I look through your pages. Stages I went through that then seemed so tragic now don't seem half as bad. I still think of myself as a sort of Jo from *Little Women*. She was a restless writer, as I am, and was a tomboy in her day. She, as well as I, never had much luck with boys, etc. Yes, Jo and I are certainly a pair.

SPRING–SUMMER 1966

MARCH 24, 1966

This time I ordered my new Beatles album from England. *Rubber Soul* has a shiny cover but a darker overall look than *Beatles VI*. The Lads aren't smiling so broadly here; their clothes are darker and their hair shaggier. Maybe they are tired of all the photographers and smiles and silly stuff. Who knows? I know I would be.

Ah, the music is still great, with more folk-rock types of arrangements on the newest album. George plays the sitar on "Norwegian Wood." That is one of my favorites, along with "Michelle," "In My Life," George's "If I Needed Someone," "Girl," and "Think for Yourself." "Nowhere Man" is totally not about love. The haunting words somehow remind me of the desperation in the lyrics of "Help!" last year.

MARCH 30, 1966

Here is yet another of my weekly columns.

Teen to Teen

By Patti

The story behind Sonny and Cher should begin in the year of 1963; for that was the year they met. Cher, a quiet girl of 17, and Sonny, a somewhat more worldly 23, discovered each other while singing as "background" voices for a recording session. According to the records, fact says that Sonny was born in Detroit, came to California while still very young and remained to become totally absorbed by anything connected with the music world. Cher, whose mother is an actress, naturally found herself drawn into the performing arts about the same time she learned to walk and talk. At first glance, one might think these two were automatically drawn together, but such was not the case. Sonny, and Cher, were and are, basically shy people and it was weeks before they found themselves on their first date. Once they talked and expressed their mutual dreams, the relationship grew for they knew that music and singing were destined to be their way of life.

Dave Clark is a young man who automatically seems to make news. Last year, for instance, he started a new craze in England when he invented a dance called the Philip Blues after the recognizable hands-behind-the-back stance of Prince Philip.

Did you know . . .

Nick Massi has left the Four Seasons and was replaced by their arranger, Charles Caletto . . . Jay and the Americans said they really hope the Hollies make it here. Jay figures they're the most underestimated group around . . . Cilla Black became engaged to, of all people, her road manager . . . Herb Alpert is one of the owners of A & H records, who release all his and the T.B. hits . . . When they started playing important night club dates, Anthony and the Imperials dropped the "little" from their names . . . Philly's own Len Barry married Hy Lit's sister-in-law on Saturday.

George Harrison is currently besieged by one particular fan who recently took an aversion to the new Mrs. Harrison and administered a good kick to her person while they were leaving a theater. The fan then got into George's Surrey home and locked him out. Following this, she climbed over his garden wall and woke him up one morning to photograph him—the print is reported to be a study in terror!

Better clear the music charts for this one "19th Nervous Breakdown" by the Rolling Stones. What is it all about? Well, as usual, it's not all that easy to get the words. But, according to Mick, the words could be directed to a society girl. It's a send-up and quite good. And Mick is quite unconcerned whether you take it as a piece of social comment or just a bit of nonsense. Most people will just take it—and play it. And so another number one is born. The Stones seem to be getting better musically. Bill Wyman's bass is great on this one—especially that descending bit at the end when the nervous breakdown arrives! Mick says about this song: "It's just something that came into my head."

Burt Ward is the young actor who plays Robin on the Batman series. He got the part because he is great in Karate and he lived across the street from one of the show's executives. Burt also was an all-star athlete in high school. By the way, Batman will start being shown by the BBC and in other European countries.

FADS IN PHILLY (AND AROUND)

In California the fad sweeping the state is bell-bottoms FOR BOYS . . . Flower printed clothes, especially skirts and matching jackets, will be big for the Shore-Set . . . Also, while sunning on the beach, don't forget your tinted "granny" glasses . . . And, of course, bring along your TIKI wood ring.

APRIL 3, 1966

I thought I would see what all the fuss was about, so last evening, a couple of us went to the Hot Shoppe at 69th Street in Upper Darby. This is the place to see and be seen on the weekends if you are a teen and either own a car or can hitch a ride with a friend. Some kids make it a doubleheader by going to the Hot Shoppe and Chez-Vous on the same evening. Basically, the Hot Shoppe is a drive-in restaurant where you park and eat in your car. Those of us poor souls without wheels hang our heads in shame and quickly duck inside the restaurant.

Three things I learned at the Hot Shoppe:

- They serve excellent burgers and fries.
- You will see at least a couple of kids you know.
- Don't disgrace yourself by not having wheels.

It started to rain as we left, and luckily we spotted a girl from our home-room driving by with her new boyfriend. They took pity on us bus-bound travelers to drive us home.

APRIL 14, 1966

All isn't too well. I am restless. Paul is still in my thoughts, but tonight my mom said that any sixteen- or seventeen-year-old was too old for the Beatles. This is the first time she ever hinted anything about my being too old to be a fan.

When she said it, all I could see was the "once happy fifteen-year-old in more joyful days." All the things I went through, and *now* to be told the farce was over. Could it be *two* long years ago that I seemed so carefree? Haven't I moved ahead in *two* years and been fooling myself? Even my Beatles pictures are turning yellow with age!

I must get unmixed somehow.

MAY 22, 1966

I have discovered that blind dates have a way of coming back at you in dark ways. My very first blind date called me and planned a visit from South Philly. Fair enough. He jumped off the bus at the wrong stop and wandered around on the back roads near the swamps. To make a long story short, not too long after his trip to Philly's Everglades, he landed in the hospital. At first, no one knew what was ailing him. Finally, his doctors diagnosed mosquito-borne viral encephalitis. Poor guy is suffering from high fevers and things I don't even want to mention here. I feel oh-so-guilty. Who would have thought?

JUNE 3, 1966

Our family said a sad farewell to Muhlfeld Street to move a few blocks away into a new townhouse on Bittern Place. It is perfect for me! Not only do I have the most adorable bedroom and new furniture but I am the proud owner of a genuine rec room. I swore to my mom that I would not paste Beatles photos over her new wallpaper. It is a small sacrifice I have to make.

Let me tell you about the rec room. It is on the ground floor at the back of our twenty-foot-wide townhouse framed by two huge sliding glass doors that open to our small yard. I decorated the rec room myself with an Island Jungle theme. The L-shaped couch is covered in a crazy leopard print, while the "bar" is also trimmed in leopard and the rocking chair is genuine bamboo. My shag carpet is an eye-popping burnt orange. To spend any time there, you will need to wear sunglasses. I can't wait to entertain my friends. Best of all, I finally have space for my stereo. I can listen to the Beatles any time, day or night. No more dirty looks from my folks in the living room as they tune in to *The Lawrence Welk Show*.

On the other hand, my new bedroom is a bit more sedate. The new antique white furniture includes a girly canopy bed and a dresser with an enormous mirror. All the better to see Patti without her braces. The desk (where my Royal Safari typewriter sits) matches the furniture and shelves. The whole look is pulled together by a royal blue rug and blue-and-white pinstripe wallpaper. I absolutely adore it.

My parents splurged on new furniture for the house. Mom decorated and Dad now has the garage of his dreams. I feel like a princess with a sparkling new home and fab furniture. Naturally, my Beatles dolls still stand proudly atop the stereo. I am sure they will enjoy the rec room as much as I will. At least I won't hear my folks complain, as the music will be blasting.

JUNE 5, 1966

I was in love! It happened late in April. I thought he was a wonderful boy. He and I got along so well—and everyone thought we were in love. He even told my girlfriends yesterday that he liked me much more than a friend. Tonight the balloon burst. He stated we were only friends and called off our dates for Friday and Saturday nights. He told me this in private. It seems so strange how one's whole composure can change from a bright, willowy girl to a down-beaten dog in a couple of sharp phrases, uttered by one you admire. My throat feels dry—my head hot—and my eyes full of tears that won't come.

Life was so beautiful until tonight, for I was loved (or thought to be) by one other than parents or dear friends. Thus I learn of life and place in my treasury of memories one slightly faded picture of a much-loved boy. Good-bye, *mon ami*. I still care, no matter what.

JUNE 15, 1966

Today we got out of school. I am now officially a senior! I can't believe it, for it seems only yesterday that I was a little eighth grader! *Tempus fugit*!

JULY 10, 1966

The Beatles goofed up with their new album cover, and the news has been over the radio and in the papers. *Yesterday . . . and Today* was first released last month with a weird cover. It was something they must have done for a joke, or perhaps they are tired of smiling in starched shirts for the cameras. Anyway, the Lads wore white lab coats and were draped in parts of baby dolls and raw pieces of meat. Not a pretty picture. The covers were recalled almost immediately—before I could run out and grab one. The replacement album cover: the Beatles, sans smiles, surround a packing trunk garbed in their usual jackets, shirts, sweaters, and even a tie!

Paul's lyrical rendition of "Yesterday," which is heard on side one, makes up for everything. Somewhere, I read he planned to call it "Scrambled Eggs." (Both *scrambled eggs* and *yesterday* have three syllables.) "Day Tripper" and "We Can Work It Out" are really great. George does a nice job on "If I Needed Someone," while Ringo's "Act Naturally" is catchy, cute, and country.

JULY 22, 1966

I am so very angry that I cannot see straight. My dad and cousin John have been teaching me to drive. I thought I was doing great, or at least OK. Driving my dad's powder blue–and–white Cadillac is gear; I especially love those electric windows. But today, Dad refused to continue with our lessons, as he said I spend too much time looking at myself in the rearview mirror and not enough time concentrating on traffic.

Men!

AUGUST 7, 1966

Oops, John really got himself in trouble now. He did an interview with reporter Maureen Cleave last March, and *Datebook Magazine* on July 31 repeated part of those quotes on the front cover. John said, "We're more popular than Jesus now." The quote was taken out of context, from what I understand, but now some radio stations in the South are banning Beatles music and calling for fans to burn their Beatles' albums, posters, and stuff. Everyone seems to be up in arms about what John said about Jesus. John has always been a free thinker. I am sure what he really meant was that the Beatles right now are more *popular* than Jesus with young teenagers. I mean, you find thousands of fans at concerts, kids waiting in lines at movie houses, and teens buying Beatles things. Unfortunately, you usually don't create the same kind of energy when it comes to teens and Christianity.

Sad, but true.

Hope John can get out of this mess.

AUGUST 10, 1966

Fashion may not be so important when you are seventeen and can't afford the latest mod designs from London, but I try to keep my *Teen to Teen* neighborhood readers up to date with the latest trends.

What's In for the Fall and Winter: Girls again will wear a variety of "Heather" colors. Poor boy sweaters will turn a new twist with differently colored horizontal ribbing added. Skirts will be short-short-short with A-line or kilt type predominating. Stockings will go even crazier with two tones very big. Also stockings of a heavy knit to match the ribbed poor boys will come on strong. Pantsuits will be the *in* item for the long winter, especially in corduroy material. These are tres chic. Low, flat, stubby heels are still predominant in the shoe line for dress, but for sport, the BABY-DOLLS in a variety of winter fabrics will make the scene. Boots will be big, but out-of-this-world styling will be a sure shot. Hair will be either very, very short or very, very long. There seems to be no in-between anymore. A different kind of look coming in is the His & Her look. This is matching outfits for boys and girls.

So sometime in the near future you and your beau might saunter up the avenue in the same corduroy pantsuits (that's if you have the nerve).

All in all, the look for this fall is neat, and good taste will prevail. So pick your wardrobe carefully, but remember last winter's clothing is still good.

AUGUST 11, 1966

John held a press conference today in Chicago where they are on tour. Part of what he said was an apology in his own John style: "I'm sorry I said it really. I never meant it to be a lousy anti-religious thing. I apologize if that will make you happy."

Oh, John, I really don't think that is going to make them happy.

AUGUST 16, 1966

BEATLES CONCERT NO. ONE. This is it! We decided to first see the Beatles on tour at JFK Stadium in Philly and then hop up to New York City next week to see them again. What could be better than that? (Maybe being Paul's girlfriend?)

Here is my *Teen to Teen* column about the concert earlier tonight, which will appear in the paper on August 31:

August 16th at J.F.K. stadium proved not as hectic as this reporter thought. The Beatles Concert only brought less than half of the 40,000 crowd that was expected. (Approximately, 21,000 fans were in the audience.)

On the bill with them were the Remains, Crykle, Ronnettes and D. Hebb. The Remains rocked through their routine first. They are quite a group and run around a lot on stage. The Cyrkle really wowed the crowd with their famous "Red Rubber Ball" and "Turn-Down Day." They also did a medley of famous songs as done by different groups such as the Beach Boys. This group looked sharp in their Black and Red striped blazers. D. Hebb, who sings the hit "Sonny," put on a one-man show with his great renditions of different songs. The Ronnettes came on from their hiding place—a truck—and sang "Be My Baby" and a few other songs. Of course, by now the audience was getting quite wild waiting for the Big B. On they came from a side dugout, guitars in hand. They got a standing ovation and it lasted for 35 minutes until they finished their show and departed in a flower truck from the stadium. The four looked pretty good in their Mod green double breasted bell bottom suits with their lime color shirts and ties.

John wore yellow-tinted round granny glasses. Three wore boots. George wore white socks and loafers. They sang such selections as "Yesterday," "If I Needed Someone," etc., etc. There were eleven songs in all. Funny but Paul seemed to ham it up the most, maybe because he is the only bachelor left—the others kind of gave him his space. Surprisingly, not too many girls screamed and the foursome could actually be heard.

With a pair of strong high-powered binoculars, they could also be seen well. All in all, it was a good concert even though this reporter could not get into the press conference.

Printed on my ticket, with four heads of the Beatles—Paul, George, Ringo, and John—all smiling:

BEATLES PRESENTED AT JOHN F. KENNEDY STADIUM
PHILA PA. AUG. 16, 1966 8:00 P.M.
UNDER AUSPICES STEEL PIER MANAGEMENT
EST. PRICE $4.76 CITY TAX .24
TOTAL $5.00 GLOBE TICKET COMPANY, PHILA.

By the way, we made a great "WE LOVE VICTOR" sign and waved it during the evening. It was a totally different feeling than the first concert back in September of 1964. No mass hysteria and less frenzy. Also, staging a concert in a massive outdoor stadium with so many fans took away a lot of that special feeling. Still, the Beatles are the Beatles, right?

Oh yeah, one of my readers sent me a letter in answer to my question "What do you think of the pop scene today?" She thinks pop music is still in but that the Liverpool sound is fading. Instead, she sees the California and Motown sounds to be more popular than ever.

AUGUST 24, 1966

BEATLES CONCERT NO. TWO. I was way too tired to write yesterday. It was a very long day in New York City. How can I possibly describe it? Well, let me scribble something down.

Diane, a couple of other Beatle Buddies, and yours truly took the train from 30th Street Station in Philly to New York bright and early. I decided to dress mod and wore a summer suit—A-line skirt and little jacket with sleeveless shell in pastel tiny flower print. Unfortunately, we decided not to take with us the "WE LOVE VICTOR" sign due to its sheer size. A Beatle

Buddy pulled out a small unopened jar of Day-Glo body paint from her handbag. As soon as she sat down on the train, she painted stars (for Ringo, naturally) all over her bare knees and then on her arms, knuckles, and hands. No, not me, as the last thing I wanted was a Day-Glo look in New York. Maybe I should have seen it coming.

We arrived in New York and slipped into the bathroom at Penn Station. Suddenly, for the first time, I noticed the *accents*. A group of girls about our age sure talked funny. I mean, it is only a couple of hours by train from Philly, but the accents really are different. I guess Brooklyn to South Philly is really a world apart.

We arrived on the streets of New York and it was hot. The city, the steamy weather and humidity, reminded me of the song "Summer in the City" by the Lovin' Spoonful, a tune that is so popular right now.

What we needed badly were cold drinks with lots of ice. We plopped ourselves down at a small refreshment stand, where the next thing I noticed was the cost of a cup of soda—forty-seven cents! That is highway robbery. Of course, we brought extra spending money just in case our train tickets would disappear. So we grudgingly dipped into our purses for coins and drank deeply from the city soft drink fountains. I really should have seen it coming.

You just knew it was Beatles concert day by the swarms of teenage fans roaming Manhattan. What else could you do until it was time to get yourself over to Shea Stadium with several thousand other kids?

On the corner, I spotted a skinny older guy. He looked faintly like the actor who stood us up in the pouring rain on Christmas Eve. Boy, he really saw us coming. We must have spelled out "Out of Town Beatlemaniacs" in Day-Glo thanks to our Beatle Buddy's colorful body artwork. He asked us if we were heading to the concert later in the day. Why on earth we answered him, I don't know. We were taught by our parents never to talk to strangers, but maybe it was our eagerness to shout out to someone that we were fans and, yes, we had our tickets.

The skinny guy waved a piece of paper in front of us. He told us in confidence that the official-looking document was an invitation to the Beatles' press conference that afternoon. We should have run right then. What we did was dig deeper into our purses to pool the twenty dollars he asked for that tantalizing slip of paper. I should have seen it coming.

Twenty dollars lighter, we searched Manhattan and found the address where the press conference was to take place. Oh, were we excited! Oh, were we dumb! To make a long story short, the piece of paper was a dud. To attend the press conference, you must present the *tickets* that were mailed with the invitation. So we stood there with a worthless paper in the middle of New York City. That bogus paper set us back twenty dollars of our hard-earned allowances.

Swindled in New York City, and all in the name of the Beatles! How could this happen to us? We really should have known better, but even the tiniest chance to see them up close at a press conference scrambled our brains.

Still, there was the Beatles concert ahead of us. I checked my ticket in my purse. There it was, just a little coupon: SHEA STADIUM ENTER GATE E. UPPER RESERVED $5.00 SEC. 35 ROW S SEAT 12. TUE., AUG. 23, 1966–7:30 P.M. SID BERNSTEIN PRESENTS (with head/upper-suited torso shots of Paul, John, George, and Ringo). NO REFUNDS—NO EXCHANGES. Who, I seriously asked myself, in her right mind, would possibly want to refund a Beatles concert ticket?

We figured out how to take the IRT subway to Shea Stadium—as crowded as you can imagine. Right there in front of us was the massive stadium, teeming with fans with banners hanging proudly throughout the arena. "Paul Is All" and "Lennon Rules" were only two of the many messages intended for our idols. You could feel the sheer energy, heat, and humidity rising as an estimated 44,600 of us fans waited in anticipation to see the Lads—our Lads. No matter if John was a bad boy, forget that George took that trip to the altar, and Paul could marry Jane any day now. They were ours for just under an hour. We had climbed and climbed until we found our top-of-the-stadium seats. Squinting through tiny binoculars, we saw them perform on a flat, bare platform stage wearing what looked like heavy military-style jackets. The temperature was somewhere in the nineties, but the Day-Glo paint never ran or smudged. Amazing stuff, that paint.

From about 9:00 to 9:50 P.M., the Beatles performed eleven songs: "Rock and Roll Music," "She's a Woman," "If I Needed Someone," "Day Tripper," "Baby's in Black," "I Feel Fine," "Yesterday," "I Wanna Be Your Man," "Nowhere Man," "Paperback Writer," and "Long Tall Sally." The acoustics here, as last week in Philly, were not bad. Fans tried to rush the stage but were stopped by security. No matter; it was unreal. The sheer numbers who were part of the Beatles family at Shea last evening made it a mystical experience.

Tired, but still excited, we took the late train back home to Philly. The show did go on, and somehow we still managed to roll along with it.

Long live the Beatles!

SEPTEMBER 1, 1966

Summer has flown its course, and I am taking my last breath of freedom before school starts. Summer wasn't too bad. I had a part-time job at the newspaper office and really enjoyed it. My hair grew longer and my tan deeper. I remember goofy things that happened. The Beatles concerts—where I saw my precious Paul.

There was no love this summer, but I didn't mind. I had fun with the whole group. The only time I felt as if I wanted to hide was when all the other girls went out on dates and I stayed home. I was all alone at times like that, but I had my Beatles records and also my good memories. Summer was good in a way. It was a summer of hope, but hoping doesn't always bring the answer. A ray of sunshine does not always bring the sun.

From work I will miss just about everyone. There was one guy who caught my eye. He is twenty years old, tall, dark, long haired, and very handsome. He works in the back room in the photography department.

We said hello, but that's it. I don't have a magnet that draws guys toward me. So many times I have tried.

So why try?

I'll miss you, my friend, but that's life!

As winter approaches, I will forget all about the summer. I must forget all the times—the good and the bad—so I can return to a normal school life. There are so many fond memories of this summer, but it's done now. As the summer breezes fade into oblivion, I shall lock my memories into my heart. Maybe they will keep until next summer. That's when I hope I'll be wiser.

AUTUMN-WINTER 1966-1967

SEPTEMBER 11, 1966

I am officially a senior in high school. Honestly, I don't know where the last few years have flown. I have grown to be a young woman, but still my mind is of a youth. I see green pastures and flowered hills. Adolescence is a trial—one of those you go through to gain insight into adulthood.

Somehow I am reaching out for something all the time—I don't know exactly what. But I must follow my mind and heart. These two things will lead me to my goal in life, whatever it is to be.

Life, I've found, is not all cotton candy, nor is it tears. It's a good mixture of both. I learned that parts of life are harder than others—and also that every dog has its day.

I still ponder some things that occurred last summer, but I'll sign off.

OCTOBER 4, 1966

So much has happened between the two concerts in August and the start of my final year in high school. I forgot to mention that the Fab Four released a super album in August. *Revolver* is different; the style is new. The Beatles explore new musical territory. Some tracks, such as "Tomorrow Never Knows" and "She Said She Said," have an out-of-this-world flavor unlike anything I have heard before. "Eleanor Rigby" has a haunting melody wrapped around some ghost-like lyrics. I love it! "Here, There and Everywhere" is simply beautiful. "Yellow Submarine" is a wild ride, while "For No One" and "Got to Get You into My Life" are more Beatles-like in lyrics and melody. All in all, this is an album to play and play again.

The cover also has a new twist. The black-and-white artwork is by the Beatles' friend Klaus Voormann. Scattered in their artistic moptops are tiny photographs. This really beats the usual album covers of unsmiling/smiling faces in dress shirts and jackets.

NOVEMBER 2, 1966

Don't see the old group much these days to talk about the Beatles. Everyone is off rushing somewhere. I cannot believe there is so much going on in senior year. Suddenly, here it is. How many will go on to college? The nuns are determined for us to apply to Catholic women's schools. Anything else is dancing with the devil. One of the good sisters referred to a secular school as "that pagan college." I am not sure what I will do. No one informed us at all about taking the SAT tests or how to apply to schools. With nearly seven hundred girls in the senior class, it is understandable that the teachers cannot cater to us all. I am thinking about Temple University for three reasons: good journalism school, inexpensive tuition, and local. I could never begin to dream about leaving Philly to attend college. Not only can my parents not afford tuition and dorms but my mom is not crazy about me attending college in the first place. No one in our family, let alone a female relative, has ever set foot in a university. In fact, not many of us graduated from high school. Even my gorgeous cousin decided to attend beauty school and skip the scholastics.

This is what Italian girls from Philly are supposed to do: develop secretarial and/or receptionist skills, take the bus to work at Bell Telephone, marry a neighborhood Italian American boy, live next door to the parents, hatch lots of grandkids quickly, and start the whole cycle over. Oh, and don't forget the obligation to cook huge family dinners each and every Sunday for the rest of your life!

Not me. This means World War III will be brewing over at my house.

Somehow, a song from the Beatles' *Revolver* album returns to haunt me. In "Eleanor Rigby," the refrain sums up nicely how I feel right at this moment.

NOVEMBER 20, 1966

Hi! Today is Sunday, and it's been some weeks since I wrote in your pages. I am on the honor roll at school. We received our school rings, and I am extremely proud of mine. The prom is in five days. I'm a little scared, because I never went to a prom before. I had a lot of trouble finding someone to go with me to the prom for *nobody cared.* All the slobs that hung around my rec room all summer somehow had excuses not to go to the prom when I asked them. Oh, I'll remember, don't worry. Finally, after asking about five boys, I finally hit upon a gem. He works in the grocery store where my mom shops. While delivering the groceries, my mom told him of my plight. He said he'd go! He is just what I've been looking for. He is nineteen, goes to Drexel Institute of Technology, and is becoming an engineer. He is also quite conservative—not wild. Doesn't smoke or drink. And he is a real gentleman. He is great for a prom, but I can't begin to think he will ask me out after. It's not my luck, as you know. It would be nice though. He is also *most handsome.* I would be happy if I would just see him in the grocery store once a week. Well, I better close and do a little homework.

NOVEMBER 26, 1966

"It was the best of times, it was the worst of times." Yes, they were the opening lines in *A Tale of Two Cities* by Charles Dickens, but he could have been writing about last night's senior prom.

The West Catholic Girls' Senior Prom, which was held in the Sheraton Hotel, left me hot and cold. Hot as in I had a great date who looked fab in a tight tux, and he could dance. Cold as in who wants to be *locked into* the Ballroom until 4:00 A.M.? Not to mention the chaperones who picked out girls wearing "revealing" gowns to banish them with instructions to cover up. Poor Mary Alice wore a short jacket the entire evening because the neckline of her green formal was branded "indecent."

Official gold and mother-of-pearl Prom Diary booklet (with fill-in-the-blank text):

The Class of 1967

WEST PHILADELPHIA

CATHOLIC GIRLS'

HIGH SCHOOL

SENIOR PROM

"Moonlight Captivation"

CHUCK GORDON

ORCHESTRA

The Sheraton Hotel Ballroom

November twenty-fifth

Nineteen Hundred Sixty-six

Dear Diary,

Tonight November 25, 1966 when we arrived at the Sheraton Ballroom, the music of the Chuck Gordon Orchestra filled us with delight.

My dress of pink velvet and peau de soie and my old-fashioned flowers matched perfectly. We danced until four o'clock. Our favorite numbers were "Gloria" and "Strangers in the Night." We were in the

Lower Balcony Room for a delicious dinner of roast beef, potatoes, string beans and baked Alaska. From one to four o'clock we stepped in time to the Misfits Band, at the best After-Prom Party I had ever had. Thrilled and tired I climbed the stairs to my bedroom at about 9 a.m. to dream of "Moonlight Captivation," the Senior Prom of the Class of '67.

DEDICATIONS

To our Parents . . . "Because of You"

To Father Nugent . . . "There Will Never Be Another You"

To our Faculty . . . "Shadow of Your Smile"

To our Escorts . . . "Cherish"

To our Chaperons . . . "Stand by Me"

To our Senior Class . . . "I'll Remember You"

To our Committee . . . "Try the Impossible"

To our Prom Night . . . "Tonight"

To our Alma Mater . . . "I Hear a Symphony"

To our School Days . . . "Yesterday"

Unofficial Patti Diary

Date: Grocery delivery boy.

Limo: 1963 maroon and black Ford Galaxy.

Dress: Sleeveless top with U-shaped neckline of passion pink velvet and long A-line skirt of white peau de soie. A white bow caught the empire waist at the middle. Ivory floor-length cloak copied from Jacqueline Kennedy's 1961 Inaugural ensemble.

Receiving Line: Introduction to principal when I nervously forgot my escort's name.

Cuisine: Raw roast beef garnished with golf-ball potatoes.

Entertainment: Line dancing, sitting on escort's lap, watching tipsy girls lose it in powder room, stuffing silverware in evening purses, and posing for "police lineup" formal photos.

Main Gripe: Prom Committee makes sure their candid photos are snapped for the upcoming yearbook's prom memories pages.

Most Fun: Diane's after-prom breakfast. So glad she invited home some of our Black friends from school and their dates. And then it was on to "bowling in a prom dress" at the Fleetwood Lanes on Elmwood Avenue.

Least Fun: 900 relatives snapping photos of my date attempting to pin my corsage.

Best of Show: Good-bye kiss in Ford Galaxy the following morning. Well worth it!

JANUARY 1, 1967

I am tired today and deserve to be, but oh, I had a perfectly wonderful New Year's Eve. This was the very first New Year's that I did not sit at home with my folks to watch Guy Lombardo on TV and yawn as the clock struck midnight. Instead, I was dressed to kill in a gorgeous short silver dress with silver ankle strap heels accented by a teeny silver bag and gloves. I am sure Jane Asher could not have looked more smashing kissing Paul under London's Big Ben on the last night of the year. It was my first time out on the biggest date night of the year, and I celebrated 100 percent. Better yet, my date was none other than my grocery boy and the once and future boyfriend.

We attended a party at some friends' of his who were recently married. Married, can you imagine? The night went way too fast: I especially enjoyed when they turned the lights down low and we danced to the slow music. I will remember that magical moment forever.

Happy New Year to all! Personally, mine got off to a spectacular start.

JANUARY 25, 1967

Teen to Teen

By Patti

In the midst of the swinging young scene, there has been a batch of young movies aimed at the IN crowd. Among these are *Morgan, The Knack, Georgy Girl* and *Alfie.* These shows are for mature audiences only and youngsters who can't comprehend what it's all about shouldn't waste their time. *Alfie* is a movie pointed at lighthearted comedy but loaded with thought. Underneath its light exterior . . . there is a real story of a man and his very mixed up life. He, being mixed up, jumbles the lives of his birds (girls). There are some very funny scenes such as the giant brawl in the pub. Michael Caine is excellent as Alfie with great performances by Shelley Winters, Murray Melvin, Jane Asher and many others.

BITS & PIECES: Dennis Wilson was so taken in by Ringo's black velvet jacket, he ordered one from tailor Dougie Millings . . . Paul McCartney (the cute Beatle, remember?) has written the film score for *The Family Way* which stars Hayley Mills . . . Quote from the new Beach Boy Bruce Johnston: "There are three types of beautiful women I like— British for variety—Californian for type—Swedish forever!" (Hey, what about us Philly birds—don't we rate?) . . . New York's Peppermint Lounge has been reopened as a disco . . . The *Peter, Paul and Mary Album*—their most recent long-playing release, is one of their greatest.

It's A-OK for the Monkees. Here's a group who are at the top and don't even play their own instruments! These four: David Jones, 20; Mickey Dolenz, 21; Mike Nesmith, 22; and Peter Tork, 22, were brought together for the first time for the TV audience. They weren't originally a group. The Monkees are here to be enjoyed—not to be picked on and prodded at, SO ENJOY THEM AND THEIR RECORDINGS. David, by the way, played in the London stage production of *Oliver* and for a while was a jockey because of his small stature.

149

Fashions for this coming year will be kooky and crazy. A top-flight English mag predicted some of the following: Plaits with nutty colored streaks . . . The East Indian type look, complete with a dot for the middle of your forehead . . . Prussian-style winter coats and high-high boots. . . . Stick on shapes and way out watches will become even more popular. . . . Girls will be wearing four inches from the hip skirts with matching tights, but fashions will drop to knee length before the year's end. . . . Clothes, shoes, stockings, bags, gloves, hair and makeup will become more colorful, with shades of violet, orange, apple green, and vivid yellow taking the lead.

Dates for area teens to remember—February 7: The Mardi Gras Teen Dance to be held in St. Barnabas School Hall, 8 to 11 P.M.—a swinging time—live music—loads of fun. Tickets at door. Come one, come all.

FEBRUARY 9, 1967

It snowed, so we were off from school on February 7 and 8. I had the strangest dream last night. I was in the play *Camelot* as Queen Guinevere. In place of the chorus was none other than the Beatles. It was like mixing the old and the new. Sort of like me—torn between old and new.

I went to another prom on Friday night. It was West Catholic Boys' High School, and a friend of a friend asked me. The guy is a champion bowler who bowls on television for prizes! Unfortunately, bowling is not a sport I'm crazy about. I find it boring, especially those awful shirts with goofy names embroidered on the back. What can I say? Farewell to the Bowling Kid. I am sure you will meet your "match" one day.

SPRING–AUTUMN 1967

APRIL 19, 1967

I don't write much about tragic news. Luckily, I have been blessed, as true sadness has not often touched my young life. Losing my Italian grandmother some years ago was about the lowest point I can remember. Standing in the windblown cemetery that November day left a void in my heart. Now, I am beginning to see sadness around me at school, even in the cafeteria, as my classmates deal with loved ones leaving to serve in Vietnam. The other day, one junior was crying at lunch. We later discovered her brother had died in the war. How could she bear it? I don't know. He was not much older than we seniors and left this world at such a tender age.

Last autumn, a number of girls brought boyfriends in uniform to the senior prom. I recall how tightly one girl hung on to her marine escort during the slow dances. I wonder where those soldiers and sailors are right now and pray for their safety. Classmates whose boyfriends are overseas often wear their bulky military rings on chains around their necks; I catch one girl in my English class unconsciously twisting her beau's ring. Perhaps it is her way to feel close to him and keep him out of danger.

This brings me to yesterday's Peace March in New York, where 125,000 protesters—led by the Rev. Martin Luther King—marched from Central Park to oppose the war. Some participants burned their draft cards, as I saw on TV last evening. The war in Vietnam is growing more and more controversial. Many of our neighborhood youths join up. Our neighborhood boys do not often attend college but instead join the military for their careers right out of high school. They are proud to be a part of the service but leave their worried parents and sweethearts behind.

What is the answer? We are trying to coming to terms with the war that is shaping our generation.

APRIL 25, 1967

My years at West Catholic are slowly coming to an end. I can tell in simple ways. The material on my uniform is now worn and shiny, while the cuffs on my long-sleeved cotton blouses are becoming frayed. I don't seem to be listening as closely to what the good sisters are advising us about our futures. We have ordered the Gleam yearbooks with our names stamped in gold lettering on the covers. Soon we will be fitted for our white caps and gowns for graduation. We seniors will host a Mother & Daughter Luncheon. Plans are in the works for our graduation Mass at the Cathedral, as well as the formal graduation ceremony at Convention Hall—the same place where I first saw John, Paul, George, and Ringo on-stage. Can you imagine that it was 1964 when I first entered Convention Hall so excited about the Beatles? Now I will end my high school years in the very same spot.

MAY 3, 1967

Teen to Teen

By Diane

Here's some news on the Beatles' new album, *Sergeant Pepper's Lonely Heart Club's Band*. Not only is it the longest album title ever put out by them, but it sounds as if it is really going to be among their best. It can be said that the Beatles have tried everything and are trying anything at least once, so no one really knows what the outcome of this record will be. No doubt with the recent influx of a sort of pop Roaring Twenties type music, the masters of experimentation will try their talents at this too. The English group, known as Sounds Incorporated, backs up one of the songs. Two records that I know of on the album are "When I Am 64" and "A Day in the Life."

MAY 14, 1967

Today is Sunday, and it is raining. That is nothing new. For the past two weeks, that is all it has been doing. I graduate from high school in a couple of weeks and cannot really believe it. It seems like yesterday I entered West Catholic, and now it is over. In between it has been so much fun with the Fab Four, Victor, and my ever-present Beatle Buddies.

I was accepted to Temple University on Good Friday. I only applied to Temple and Philadelphia Community College but had my heart set on the former. Temple U. is a major university situated in the heart of North Philly and only a short ride from home on public transportation. Temple is known for its School of Communication, where I hope to study journalism later this year. The "J" School is neatly tucked away in an old brownstone on North Broad Street. I am looking forward to this experience, although it is a bit scary. The thought of me as a college freshman actually petrifies me. Math never was a strong subject, and it is a required course in the first year. Oh, well . . .

MAY 29, 1967

Today at 3:15 P.M. the graduation caps and gowns were distributed to all seniors after we paid our five dollar deposit. To see the wonderful white gowns with gold and blue hoods up close and touch the tassels of our caps is a feeling I cannot even begin to describe. Now, we start nearly two weeks of rehearsals for our Baccalaureate Mass and the graduation at Convention Hall. I am sure the ceremony will be a lot more dignified than a Beatles concert.

The nuns won't ease up on us just because we are graduating. Oh, no, our two-page Commencement Schedule for the Class of 1967 is very detailed and restrictive. EVERY GIRL MUST REPORT IN FULL UNIFORM (STOCKINGS INCLUDED) AND ON TIME FOR REHEARSAL.

Below I have listed only some of the instructions:

Do not pin corsages on the hood. . . . Pin tassel left front. Use a white hatpin, if necessary, not bobby pins, to secure cap. Wear the mortar board straight. Do not alter the gown without Sister's permission. Wear a long shadow-panel slip, short white gloves and white shoes. . . . Keep gown and hood free from lipstick smears. Pin hood underneath at each shoulder.

By 9 A.M. Monday, June 12, your Homeroom Sister must have every gown. Return the hood and gown in the same box you received them. . . . Our contract expires at 10 A.M. Anyone who has not returned hers will get a bill for her gown and hood. . . . You will be fined $1 for each hour after 9 A.M. you have not returned your gown and hood.

Baccalaureate Mass: Go to confession in your own parish on Saturday, June 3. On Tuesday, June 6, report directly to the assigned assembly point at the Cathedral. Do not loiter on the steps, or in the street. Only the school photographer may take pictures in the Cathedral. Please advise your parents of this. Wear a rubber band on your arm for your gloves and your Mass leaflet.

Graduation: On Sunday evening, June 11, use the side or back doors of Convention Hall. Do not use front entrance. No girl is to enter the main auditorium until she does so officially in the academic procession. There are no means of distributing flowers or telegrams at Convention Hall on Graduation Day. Be sure that your parents and friends direct their congratulations and gifts to your home.

General: Wear the school uniform and *stockings* to every rehearsal. *Chewing gum* and *make-up are forbidden.*

This was only part of our instructions. During rehearsals, we were told to SIT DOWN: DO NOT STAND IN THE AISLES AT ANY TIME and to "Report in *silence* . . ."

No fooling around at West Catholic. Not even in the final few days as a senior.

JUNE 6, 1967

After endless rehearsals, running to confession, painstakingly fixing my cap and gown, and arriving to the Cathedral of Sts. Peter and Paul at 18th and Race Streets, I was ready to report in *silence* at 9:15 A.M. The 10:00 A.M. Mass with seniors singing the Ordinary of the Mass, while the choir sung the Proper, went off without a hitch. Except for experiencing the worst case of cramps in recent memory, it was a day to remember.

JUNE 11, 1967

At long last—my graduation. Earlier tonight, my family and friends gathered in our living room on Bittern Place, placed long-stemmed roses in my arms, gave me words of encouragement, and snapped my photo. Don't know why, but I felt rather serious. Perhaps the enormity of the whole thing is finally hitting my pea-sized brain. Our homeroom nuns gave out the diplomas before the ceremony at Convention Hall, and we hid them under our gowns. What a feeling to hold four years of blood, sweat, and tears close to my heart. The 8:00 P.M. academic procession was rather long. I was afraid my father would fall asleep and start snoring. Our commencement speaker pontificated on "Love." According to the words of wisdom in our

Gleam yearbook, "THE WORLD IS OURS. Commencement at Convention Hall is the culmination of four years of spiritual development, academic achievement and social maturity. With this attained, the graduates strive to choose the right path that makes 'all the difference.'"

OK, if the world is ours, where and how do I sign up for ownership?

JUNE 17, 1967

This Saturday brought luck, as it happened to be the final day of Our Lady of Loreto's annual church carnival. Everybody knows the empty lot on the hill is always the perfect spot to view the fireworks from inside your date's '63 Galaxy.

"Maybe I'll meet you at the carnival tonight over by the grocery store, maybe about 8:30 before the start of the procession and fireworks," he said when he delivered the cartons of groceries earlier today.

This was my chance.

The shoes hurt. That was the first thing I noticed as I set off for Woodland Avenue later—at least two hours early for my grocery store rendezvous, and against my mom's wishes. I wore my crisp white sundress and felt overdressed, as the carnival crowd is more into sneakers and shorts. The long hike to the carnival made my white patent leathered feet scream in outrage. There was some relief after I bought Band-Aids and then comforted myself with a black-and-white ice cream soda at Theodore's Restaurant.

Finally, dusk fell, and I strolled very casually down the block fronting the small parish church. Carnival sights and sounds floated around me: "Win a teddy bear," "Hot pizza downstairs." The colored bulbs danced in the breeze to the music of the merry-go-round. Popcorn crunched under my feet while the band played on and on. The carnival's final hours gave off energy of their own as if it couldn't give up until next summer.

But would *he* be there?

I walked down one more block to where the heat and noise were less intense. There, parked by the store, was a Mr. Softee Ice Cream truck tinkling its familiar tune. Around the back of the truck, his foot up on the bumper, he was engaged in conversation with the neighbors. No delivery boy attire this evening; he wore a sharp madras button-down shirt paired with freshly ironed chino slacks. He looked up through a wisp of hair caught on his forehead and spotted me in the crowd. His dark eyes spoke volumes.

It was our night for fireworks.

JUNE 18, 1967

Still have not caught my breath from last night, but yes, I really did graduate high school last week. Before I know it—I'll be a college freshman! Needless to say, I can't believe how swiftly the time flies. Yesterday (or so it seems), I was an insecure eighth grader not knowing the world about me. Today, although I am still mixed up, I feel a little more sure of myself. Growing up is a long, complicated affair.

Well, happy twenty-fifth birthday, Paul McCartney—I still love you, although we both have been through a lot!

JUNE 30, 1967

I just returned from the Student Workshop at Temple University. It was held for three and a half days to acquaint us with college life. I met interesting people all around the campus and got to know other freshmen in the few days I was there. There were so many students from the area Catholic high schools, which surprised me. I lived in the dorms with a roommate, and that was a fun experience, since in reality I will continue living at home during my college years. We learned a bit of what college life will be like while we explored the campus and learned to identify the buildings. Now I can tell Mitten Hall from Baptist Temple. Suddenly, Temple U. doesn't seem foreign, as I have had an insider's look. The campus is urban, yet inviting. While a group of us were sitting around talking, we heard the news that actress Jayne Mansfield was killed in a horrific car accident. This was very shocking news during an otherwise exciting time for us on campus.

I am staring at my new official Temple U. ID card. I, no. 119805, appear dazed in the small photo on the right, not like a sophisticated college coed at all. My pale blue headband has a tiny bow on top reminiscent of Snow White. I must remember to ditch that bow on campus. It is great, though, to see the words "TEMPLE UNIVERSITY" and the school seal at the top of the ID card in bold red letters. The word STUDENT also appears in red and almost jumps out at me just in case I don't know who I am and why I am there. I feel as if I am on my way—somewhere . . . somehow . . .

Coming home at 13th Street and carrying my heavy suitcase, I met none other than my prom date waiting for a trolley, too. Well, I did wait ten minutes until I saw him. He didn't talk very much. Perhaps he'd had an off day. Hmmm, it sure is easier understanding Paul McCartney.

SEPTEMBER 12, 1967

I was quite worried about entering college until two minutes ago. That's when I discovered something I wrote on March 22, 1963. It was right before I entered high school and took my placement test. I quoted Roosevelt by saying, "The only thing we have to fear is fear itself." Now I am not frightened as I was before. Somehow I'll be strong, and with good ol' F.D.R., I'll make it. If I stay calm, everything will be OK next week.

OCTOBER 20, 1967

What can I say about my first weeks at Temple University? It is baffling to be in a school with thousands of students and so many confusing assignments, new teachers, and tucked-away classrooms. My classes are scattered over campus, which means I have to walk long distances. The rhythm of college is so new to me: buying textbooks, taking detailed notes, waiting in endless lines, and even finding decent places to eat lunch. The best thing I can do right now is to learn my way around, keep up with assignments, and meet others like me. My course load is typically first year for a liberal arts student planning on a journalism major: Journalism 002, Society and Mass Communications; English 01, Composition; History 01, History of Western Civilization; Math 001, Introduction to Modern Math; Sociology 001, Introduction to Sociology; and HYPER 001, Fundamentals of Physical Education.

To get me through all this, I added some great pieces to my wardrobe—a beige corduroy suit, a leather jumper, and a six-button velour pantsuit. Then I felt incredibly overdressed as I discovered the fashion style is casual on campus. Jeans and sweaters are more the norm than Ivy League button-down shirts, V neck sweaters, and pleated skirts. I seem to be the only girl wearing a skirt to classes. One long-haired guy in my math class likes to sit there passing the time by coloring in the white stripes on his bell-bottoms with blue pen. He wears the same leather vest to every class coupled with worn motorcycle boots. He reminds me of rocker Jim Morrison. I secretly dubbed him "Electric Factory," which is the name of a local rock club.

Did I mention that I met a nice guy during orientation? He is a freshman from South Philly who plans to become a pharmacist. We ride to school together when we both have early-morning classes and then hang around on campus. My English class with a seasoned professor is at 8:30 sharp. She taught comedian Bill Cosby a few years ago. My nice guy is studious with a wicked sense of humor. He reminds me a bit of *Superman's* Clark Kent with his square-framed glasses. During the summer, we found ourselves on Chestnut Street in Center City waiting to see a movie when we heard the Beatles' *Sgt. Pepper* album blaring from the open door of the new head shop selling black light posters, incense, beads, and peace buttons. We both agreed that the Beatles are still everywhere, even on an evening out in Center City.

Believe it or not, I also won a contest on radio station WFIL. My postcard was picked from a barrel, and I became the winner of an evening on the town: a chauffeured Cadillac limousine for the night and dinner for two at the Matr' D Restaurant. I asked my grocery boy/prom date to be my escort, and we went out on August 19—a Saturday night. A funny thing happened on the way to dinner. He asked the limo driver, who, by the way, was also a singer in a Philly soul group, to go slowly past the grocery store. When we cruised past, his dad was sitting outside and did a double take when he saw his son wave from a fancy limo. Wish I had a camera!

His dad told him the following day that the limo made him nervous. He had a strange feeling that his quiet son may have hired a limo to elope.

By the way, on Thursday, August 31, we went out again. This time we saw the newest James Bond film—*You Only Live Twice* with Sean Connery—at the drive-in. Mr. Bond is so popular!

NOVEMBER 26, 1967

It is funny what life does to you. . . . A few minutes ago, I heard "Love Me Do" played on the radio. Immediately, my heart skipped a beat, and it was February 1964 again. The early Beatles record brought back many thoughts and intense feelings. Suddenly, a flood of memories and a certain excitement hit me hard.

Of course, the Beatles aren't the only focal point of my life now, but they have played an important part in my past. They actually helped me to grow up and lose my shyness. Before they emerged upon the scene, I was the perfect bookworm. During Beatlemania, I blossomed into a regular teen who loved rock 'n' roll and Paul McCartney. (I still really admire Jamie.)

In the future, if someone states that "the Beatles were good for nothing," I'll smile, for I know the truth. They were part of a spellbinding phenomenon that pushed me out from my little corner and into the big world. For this, I shall always be thankful.

PART II

INTERVIEWS

OUR MUSE
ALL WE NEED IS VICTOR SPINETTI

We loved Victor for his wit, charm, compassion, distinctive ski slope nose, and wonderful tales of John, Paul, George, and Ringo.

Although a renowned star of stage and screen, he gently befriended hoards of teenage Beatles fans who hyperventilated at his feet. Thanks to his winning personality, you could not help but adore this remarkable man for himself. Victor was an enigma: an actor and bon vivant, yet 100 percent approachable. This is what made him so yummy. Victor would brighten a day just by being Victor. In fact, Paul McCartney said it best when he described him as "the man who made the clouds disappear."

This versatile actor, writer, director, and raconteur was raised in the mining town of Cwm, Wales, by Italian Welsh parents. After attending Cardiff's College of Music and Drama, he developed a comedy act and later was invited by Joan Littlewood to join her company, Theatre Workshop. Victor received the prestigious Théâtre des Nations award in Paris in 1963 (which he shared with *King Lear*'s Paul Scofield) for his right-on MC and

Sergeant Major roles in Littlewood's *Oh What a Lovely War*. Victor was also the recipient of the 1964 Tony Award for his roles in the Broadway production of *Oh What a Lovely War*. The Beatles invited him to be part of their loopy ensemble, and he romped through all their films. Along the way, he appeared in a host of classics, such as Franco Zeffirelli's *The Taming of the Shrew* (1967) with Elizabeth Taylor and Richard Burton, *The Return of the Pink Panther* (dir. Blake Edwards, 1975) starring Peter Sellers, and *Voyage of the Damned* (dir. Stuart Rosenberg, 1976) featuring Orson Welles and Faye Dunaway. As an eminent director, Victor directed Andrew Lloyd Webber's *Jesus Christ Superstar* in Paris; John Lennon's *In His Own Write*; and James Rado, Gerome Ragni, and Galt MacDermot's *Hair* in Rome and Amsterdam.

Victor's stage, screen, and television credentials can fill a book. In fact, *Victor Spinetti Up Front . . . : His Strictly Confidential Autobiography*, which was published in 2006, delightfully dishes up what went on behind the scenes in his long career and chronicles his close encounters with a bevy of Broadway and cinema celebs: Sean Connery, Marlene Dietrich, Joan Crawford, Mel Brooks—to name only a few.

Victor was like a fine wine: he only got better with age. On the sunny side of the millennium, he appeared in a number of TV series and stage productions—*Albert's Boy* (2005) as Albert Einstein; at the London Palladium, *Chitty Chitty Bang Bang* (2002) as the Baron; *The Merry Widow*; *The Tempest*—and toured around the United Kingdom in several productions as he entered his eighties. Never one to forget his fans from the Swingin' Sixties, Victor frequently popped in at Beatles happenings, such as the Fest for Beatles Fans in the United States, where he enchanted audiences with his tales of the Liverpool Lads.

VICTOR UP CLOSE AND PERSONAL

Victor Spinetti needed no introduction to this group. Those who attended the Fest for Beatles Fans in Las Vegas in 2007 recognized him on sight—despite the passage of four decades. Almost from the moment he was introduced, the crowd became mesmerized. Nattily attired in a dark polo and scarf, the septuagenarian actor charmed audiences with tales of John, Paul, George, and Ringo. In the wake of his interview with the moderator, he explained his philosophies on life.

We later sat down to talk in his simple Vegas hotel room. In an hour's time, Victor would once again take center stage. And after, he gallantly signed autographs and smiled and posed for photos with dozens of fans who had waited in line to share in the magic of a very special era.

The Victor I knew in the mid-1960s was approachable and benevolent. He somehow always made time for us youngsters. Though we had not seen one another since rock was king, he remained the same down-to-earth Victor. Staring across the table at one of his own flock, I was curious to discover what he thought of the adulation of the teenage girls who eagerly followed him after he appeared in *A Hard Day's Night*. How did he remain upbeat to these constant pilgrims?

"I know how it feels to actually yearn after someone that you love and you probably will never ever meet," Victor explained. "When I was young I used to love Flash Gordon . . . Rita Hayworth. Oh, God, how wonderful. But I never met them. I finally met someone and said, 'You *know* them. Tell me about them.' I can understand that. And that is why I did it and that is why I still do it.

"If someone says, 'You mean you were there—tell us about it.' Well, give it away. If you have a memory, channel it any way you like. You can do it in an interview, do it on television or in a book. But you get rid of it. You give it away and it is yours forever. I know what it is to long for someone . . . to know something about someone. At that time—when I was first there—hardly anybody knew anything about them. They knew them as the Beatles, but they all looked the same in a way. I received a letter from their manager, Brian Epstein, and the boys all signed it and wrote 'Thanks for the plug in New York.' I don't know where that letter is today. It is probably gone."

Sincerely

Peter Smith

I was curious about his first impressions on meeting John, Paul, George, and Ringo. What surprised him about the Beatles? He was thoughtful, and his eyes grew wide. "I loved them. I was a fan. If I could have screamed, I would have. They were delicious. I mean that they were truly unique."

One of the things Victor pointed out to the audience was that during filming with the Beatles, he marveled at their intellectual conversations. "Can you imagine sitting with today's musicians and discussing Freud, Jung, Matisse, or René Magritte? We talked about impressionism. These people were seekers," he elaborated. "They wanted to know things—John in particular and George, too. Ringo—he was complete. He didn't need to find out anything. He knew everything already," he joked.

Meanwhile, Victor worked steadily with the group in *A Hard Day's Night, Help!,* and *Magical Mystery Tour.* He also directed Lennon's *In His Own Write* for the stage. "If I had to pick favorites, I would choose the TV director's role in *A Hard Day's Night,*" he said. "Also, the sergeant major role I did every night on stage in London in *Oh What a Lovely War.* When John saw me do that, he wanted me to repeat the role in *Magical Mystery Tour.* They also asked me to play the role of the courier on the bus, but I would have had to travel with them on the Magical Mystery tour. Since I was on the stage, I already had an obligation."

Much has been made of their impact on the world of pop culture as the Beatles shine brightly in the stratosphere, along with Elvis. "At the time, I just felt that I was in the magic circle, and I am still in it." Victor elaborated, "George had once written out the words for me to 'Tomorrow Never Knows' as I told him that I couldn't hear them clearly on the record—'Relax and float down stream . . .' Some friends came to my home and I gave the piece of paper to them. This one friend—a famous American—said to me, 'In ten years no one will know who they are.'"

Were the Beatles aware of their devoted fan base long after they disbanded? "In 1980, I asked Paul if he would like to come with me to look at Beatle Fest. I happened to be with Paul and Linda at the time. Paul turned to me and questioned, 'Will anybody turn up?' And I said, 'Why don't you come?' He looked across to Linda and then shook his head. Paul and Ringo may show up one of these days. Let's set the stage for their return."

Victor looked back on his long, colorful career as an actor fondly remembering the international stages and sets on which he worked. He reminisced, "If I had a time machine, I would love to return to Rome with Elizabeth Taylor and Richard Burton on the set of *The Taming of the Shrew.*"

Filming in Rome, they had a wonderful time. It was the most extraordinary place, thanks to Liz and Dick. Not only did Liz enjoy pitching in to do makeup for the extras but she volunteered to help with Victor's makeup as well. The Burtons chartered a bus for the cast to attend a barbecue, where they flew in food from Nathan's in New York. Chef Elizabeth, who glistened with sweat, was in charge of the grill.

Time after time, Victor appeared with the legends of stage and screen. He rubbed elbows and shared friendships with such icons as Marlene Dietrich. Whether playing the role of Felix in Neil Simon's 1965 classic *The Odd Couple* on the London stage or taking his turn as an eminent director in the capitals of Europe, Victor has seen them all—and worked with the best.

He grinned. "If I could, I would wish to work once again with Orson Welles. He was wonderful. During filming, he said, 'This scene is about Victor. It is not about my character. So the camera should be on Victor and not on me.' He was most generous. He would say, 'Give me strength. Give me strength.' Yes, I certainly would like to work with Orson again, and Richard Burton and Elizabeth Taylor. Richard was also a most generous man. He once wrote a letter in my behalf to the U.S. immigration authorities. It said, 'Victor Spinetti is most trustworthy. The only thing he has ever stolen from me is a scene.' I didn't keep it. I don't know where it is." He shook his head sadly.

Victor's long career as an actor delighted audiences for more than a half-century. Not only did he still perform with gusto into his eighties but he offered pearls of wisdom during his chats with fans and in his popular one-man performances. At the Fest for Beatles Fans, he explained with a dramatically sweeping gesture, "If you want something, you should give it away. Give away the important things. Love, truth, humanity, warmth, and generosity. All things that make life worth living, you give away. And they are yours forever."

———

Sadly, Victor Spinetti left us on June 18, 2012, at the age of eighty-two in his native Wales. On October 2, 2012, Sir Paul McCartney paid an impromptu tribute to Victor at the actor's memorial service held at St. Paul's Church in Covent Garden, London.

AND HERE'S HYSKI
PHILLY'S OWN DEEJAY
BEHIND THE BEATLES

The name "Hy Lit" is synonymous with rock 'n' roll radio. As the voice of Philadelphia radio for more than a half-century, Hy (also known as Hyski O'Roonie Mcvoutie O'Zoot) was a warm and fuzzy voice on the radio. Hy was not only family in Philly but a genuine piece of pop music history owing to his long and illustrious career. The concerts Hy had emceed read like the who's who of rockdom: the Beatles, Elvis, the Rolling Stones, the Beach Boys, the marvelous Motown groups, and so many more.

One of the East Coast's most renowned deejays, Hy started out in 1954. Not only was he the number one jock on WIBG, the city's AM powerhouse during the height of the rock 'n' roll era, but Hy also hosted TV shows in Philadelphia and syndicated shows in Detroit, Cleveland, and San Francisco.

He dominated the airwaves in Philadelphia for decades, at WIBG and Oldies 98.1 FM, and won countless awards through the years. His knowledge of music and the music business was phenomenal. Voted

173

"Most Handsome Deejay in the World" in 1967, Hy's thirty-five-thou-
sand-member fan club knew he was the cutest—and most talented—guy
on radio.

I had the privilege to interview Hy Lit and Sam Lit at their Philadelphia
cyber radio station, Hylitradio.com, in summer 2006.

THE BEATLEMANIA GOSPEL ACCORDING TO HY

"She Loves You Yeah Yeah Yeah" and the Beatles were born. I walked out of the radio station one evening in December after doing my show and I saw something on my windshield—the letters "B" and "E." So I thought nothing of it. Tore up the piece of paper and threw it away. The day after that there was an "A," followed by a "T" the next day. Each morning another letter was added. By the end of the week, the message was complete—the Beatles are coming!

The last day there was a record on my windshield. I was curious enough to go back to the station to listen to it. In those days I received hundreds of records, but was curious about this one. The gimmick they were using was creating curiosity. I listened, and didn't think too much of it. I thought it was a good record. No big thing. Soon I received phone calls from teenagers hearing about the Beatles. They wanted to hear their music. They never heard of them. So, I went on the air to tell this story "the Beatles are coming." I played the record and suddenly the phone lines lit up. I was totally in shock to see how many people knew about the Beatles, but hadn't heard them yet.

It was a very good publicity stunt.

The Beatles became the hottest thing in the world. So hot they were white hot. That is how hot they were back then. I decided to bring them to Philly. I went to the William Morris Agency in New York. I visited New York purposely to book the Beatles. They wanted a $25,000 certified check. I called an automobile dealer I knew and said that I need $25,000. I wanted him to become my partner and invest twenty-five grand in the new group called the Beatles. I told him that this was going to be something great. I said if I don't get the Beatles now, I am not going to get them.

With certified check in hand, I walked into the William Morris Agency and sat down. There were three or four other people competing to bring the Beatles to Philadelphia. I said that I was a disc jockey and they answered that they knew who I was. I joked that I would seek revenge if I didn't get them into the city. "You don't have $25,000, do you?" I answered, "Put your money where your mouth is."

Philadelphia police commissioner Frank Rizzo (who later became mayor) and I arranged to have the Beatles smuggled in from Atlantic City, New Jersey, by a Hackney's fish truck. While a decoy limousine drove up the New Jersey White Horse Pike, the fish truck with the Beatles took the Black Horse Pike and drove past thousands of screaming fans into the food service entrance at Philadelphia Convention Hall on September 2, 1964.

BEATLE HEADACHES AND 7-UP FIZZES

Hy and fellow deejay Joe Niagara first met the Fab Four in February 1964 at a swanky "Meet the Beatles" cocktail reception at the Plaza Hotel in New York. That is when it dawned on Hyski that the Beatles had to be his when they hit the concert stages in the United States later that year, in September.

Here is a capsule of what occurred in those early days of Philadelphia Beatlemania according to Hy's son Sam Lit:

Within weeks the Beatles appeared on *The Ed Sullivan Show,* which commands a Super Bowl–sized viewership, and overnight America fell hard for the Fab Four. Tickets went on sale in May, starting at $2.50 for nose-bleed seats and topping out at $5.50 for the floor. Philadelphia Convention Hall's thirteen thousand seats sold out in ninety minutes. A mini riot ensued when word of the sellout reached the scores of Beatlemaniacs still in line for tickets. Hyski was hit up with so many VIP won't-take-no-for-an-answer ticket requests that when it was over and the Beatles left town, he was out $5,000.

In fact, the whole thing turned out to be an incredibly big headache. The suits at the station gave him guff about the stunt he pulled on a *Bulletin* reporter who was writing trash about Beatles fans the day of the ticket sales. Hyski announced the reporter's phone number on air and told listeners to call him up and scream in his ear. The *Bulletin* reporter complained to his boss, who then turned around and gave Hy's boss an earful when they were out on the back nine together. At which point, the boss came back to the clubhouse and phoned Hyski to say he was off the air for a couple of days without pay.

On top of that, Hyski was getting static from 7-Up, one of the station's biggest sponsors. They were demanding exclusive pouring rights for the concert through the station. Hyski told Mr. 7-Up no. He didn't need this crap from some soda jerk; he cordially invited 7-Up to shove it. They then threatened to stop all soda sales. Hyski said, "So what, you ever heard of water?" Well, the station brass wanted to suspend him for that too, but Hyski wasn't having it. He was untouchable, and he knew it. He reminded them that he took a bullet for the team back in 1960 when payola hit the fan and he was off the air briefly. Now he was done taking bullets. He wasn't interested in yet another vacation. "You suspend me, I'll resign and take the Beatles with me," he said. And that was the end of that.

"I enjoyed the Beatles very much. Their success was amazing. Their music was and still is fantastic. They played a big role in my career," Sam concluded.

HY NAMED IT THE HOTTEST TICKET IN THE WORLD

Fans called the station—the lines lit up like a Christmas tree. The only fans who were mad at me were the ones who cut school to go down to Convention Hall to buy tickets and they were sold out—sold out—sold out! They were in tears. The fans were mad at me because they thought I dirty tricked them. They took it personal because the tickets sold out. I had so many people calling me for tickets. They were all putting pressure on me. I had a hundred tickets for VIPs, but I went from a thousand tickets to one hundred in a single day. It was the hottest ticket in the world.

The Beatles sent a long list of what they wanted, and the William Morris Agency forwarded it to me a week before the concert. They wanted cots and soft blankets to take naps in their dressing room. Oh, and fish and chips and Scotch and Coca-Cola.

The most interesting thing was when I met Paul McCartney and he said, "I say, what *is* a Hy Lit?"

And then they asked for the worst drink in the world—rum and Coca-Cola.

It was easily the most amazing night of my life. I walked out on that stage with the fans screaming and hollering. I thought, "Have your fun screaming and hollering." But we didn't hear much of the Beatles.

I loved the Beatles. They were great guys. I didn't like those folks who managed them, but that is another story.

Can this phenomenon ever repeat itself? It will happen again at some point in time. Perhaps he is working in a gas station or library right now. But certainly there will be another super star. I remember when I first met Elvis. I just know the way the cameras were popping that he was going to be a star. I shook hands with him and his fingers were icy cold. Even the great Elvis was nervous before he got up there on that stage.

———

The legendary seventy-three-year-old deejay Hy Lit died on November 17, 2007, and his legacy has been passed down to his son Sam.

IS THERE LIFE AFTER BEATLEMANIA?

At about the same time my high school years were drawing to a close, I came to realize that running after the Beatles was akin to a puppy chasing its tail—all bark and no bite. It was fun, it gave me a focus, but ultimately it produced exhaustion and frustration. The dawning of this understanding signaled a change in me and, indeed, a change in the world I inhabited.

Although the Lads were no longer the focal point of my life, I still adored Beatles music and collected their phenomenal albums as I went about my new life as a university freshman in my hometown. During my college career and down through the years, I closely followed the group and its members' careers and milestones. With millions, I mourned the untimely deaths of John Lennon and George Harrison, events that marked the end of the dream for me and many others. Although I had grown and come to know that things do change, the Beatles nonetheless earned a place of honor in my heart, where they remain to this day. Through the years, nothing or no one has ever shaken my devotion to the Fab Four.

Glancing at the wall above my desk, three colorful Beatles movie posters smile down on me and my family. This is a gentle reminder that merges past and present in our household. Naturally, Beatlemania has been a rite of passage for the next generation, as my twin daughters Jane and Margaretha have been sprinkled with the magic of the mania. Among their early memories is dance time with Mommy, jumping up and down to Beatles tunes. Music and more music flooded the car as I paid my dues through the soccer-mom years. The car pool proved a perfect excuse to review all the Beatles CDs as we motored through the twins' formative years to Scout meetings, sports lessons, and school. It was also my solemn duty as a Beatlemaniac mom to escort my brood to concerts when Paul or Ringo landed a gig in our town. The fact that my girls will be able to tell their children and grandchildren that they actually saw Paul and Ringo live on stage gladdens the heart of this old fan.

Speaking of old fans, some of my Beatle Buddies remain friends after several decades. Unfortunately, others have completely disappeared from my radar, and some, sadly, have passed on. More than half a century is a long time. Actor Victor Spinetti kept in touch until his death. He was

such a marvelous, charming gentleman, and he is missed. Deejay Hy Lit also kept me in the loop, and since his untimely passing, his son Sam has graciously stepped in. Hy Lit is dearly missed by so many fans through the halls of rock 'n' roll.

We all learned Liverpool slang words such as "luv," "fave," and "gear." We devoured information published in fan magazines about George's collar size and frantic Beatle romances. I hosted birthday parties every June 18 for an ever-absent Paul. The long-distance calls to Liverpool never quite made it. When both George and Ringo were married, we watched over the red-eyed members of our group.

It took us time to realize that we weren't getting responses to our fan letters and that the scatterbrained meeting plans wouldn't work. And if we had met them, what then? We never made any long-range postcapture plans. It was the chase to meet them that excited us.

We never made it.

But was Beatlemania only a passing teenage fancy to grow out of and get over? This was nothing new: frantic Elvis fans paid homage in the 1950s, while Frank Sinatra's bobby-soxers swooned in the 1940s. In the 1920s, women fans fainted when Rudolph "The Sheik" Valentino appeared on the silver screen. A crowd of one hundred thousand gathered outside the funeral home when Valentino died at thirty-one in August 1926.

Undoubtedly, each fan experience was different. Because we were so young, so innocent and impressionable, Beatlemania left its mark on many of us far beyond the pure love of the music. In my life, the Beatlemania phenomenon was a positive force—in ways my parents and teachers could not have fathomed or foreseen. Beatlemania helped me stumble through the halls of adolescence and tumble into adulthood. I lost my shyness, became more assertive, blossomed into a social butterfly, launched a fledgling writing career, developed administrative and managerial skills, and, most importantly, gained a newfound independence. I don't think that college, although it was a much-needed milestone, could have accomplished all that for me.

No, I cannot speak for others, but I do know firsthand that Beatlemania was a lifeline for some fans. One of my Beatle Buddies lost a parent in the midst of the frenzy. She doesn't know how she would have survived that awful period without the "support" of the Liverpool Lads. Yet another Beatle Buddy lived in a dysfunctional family. To her, Beatlemania was the breath of fresh air that made her teen years bearable. It helped her get through the lows to gather strength and spirit.

What still can be heard loud and clear after so many decades is, simply, the music. The music was the message from the Beatles at the very beginning and remains so today. Timeless tunes are as fresh in the twenty-first century as they were barely two decades after World War II. Young and old can appreciate the pure harmonies and witty lyrics. This music lives on, whether interpreted by world-class symphony orchestras or spirited school marching bands. Listen carefully to the haunting "The Long and Winding Road" and "Things We Said Today" or the retrospective "In My Life." Beatles songs stand the test of time. We can still laugh at "Yellow Submarine," "Ob-La-Di, Ob-La-Da," and "The Continuing Story of Bungalow Bill"; share John's anxiety in "Help!" and "Nowhere Man"; or feel funky listening to "She's Leaving Home" and "Eleanor Rigby." Then there are the feel-good songs, such as "Good Day Sunshine," "All You Need Is Love," and "Hello, Goodbye." Imagine how young they were when they penned "When I'm Sixty-Four," and appreciate their early taste for nostalgia in "Penny Lane." If love is eternal, then Beatles songs reign supreme.

In my diary, I summed up my feelings on November 26, 1967, when I wrote, "Of course, the Beatles aren't the only focal point of my life, but they have played an important part in my past. They actually helped me to grow up and lose my shyness. . . . In the future if someone states that 'the Beatles were good for nothing,' I'll smile, for I know the truth. They were part of a spellbinding phenomenon that pushed me out from my little corner and into the big world. For this, I shall always be thankful."

SUBJECT INDEX

Page numbers in italics contain photographs.

mention in Philadelphia, 24; growing popularity of, 4, 26–27, 29; legacy of, 6, 160, 181; long-distance calls by Beatles Buddies to, 40, 121, 181; slang used by, 9, 37–38, 181; Victor Spinetti's stories of, 165, 166, 167, 169; wives and girlfriends, 34, 44, 83–84, 90, 104, 119, 123, 129, 181. *See also* concerts, Beatles; contests, Beatles; *Ed Sullivan Show,* Beatles appearances on [in Title Index]; souvenirs, Beatles

Beehan, Pauline, marries Gerry Marsden, 91

Beverly: O.V.S.F.C.A. secretary, 64; selling Beatles buttons, 29, 31

Black, Cilla, 92, 129

Black, Terry, 92

Blavat, Jerry (deejay), 117

Boyd, Pattie: in *A Hard Day's Night,* 52, 84; marries George, 123, 129, 181

boys, 18, 19, 21, 140–41. *See also* Patti, dates

Brambell, Wilfrid, 122

bubblegum cards, Beatles, 9, 31, 107–8. *See also* souvenirs, Beatles

Buchwald, Art, backlash after Beatles criticism, 29

Burton, Richard, 166, 170

buttons, Beatles, 29, 31, 46, 52 *See also* souvenirs, Beatles

Byrds, 124–25

C

Caine, Michael, in *Alfie,* 149

Caletto, Charles, 129

Carol: attending *A Hard Day's Night* movie, 45; O.V.S.F.C.A. charter member, 64

Chad & Jeremy, 85

Charles, Prince of Wales, Patti's crush on, 20

Cher. *See* Sonny and Cher

Chez-Vous Ballroom, 117–18, 131

Clark, Dave, 129. *See also* Dave Clark Five

Clark, Gene, 124–25

Clark, Petula, 85–86

Ronnettes, performing at 1966 Philadelphia concert, 136

Rosenberg, Stuart, 166

Rydell, Bobby, 86

S

Scofield, Paul, 165

Sellers, Peter, 166

Shaw, Sandy, 109

Shindig! road show, 102

Sinatra, Frank, 28, 76, 183

slang, Beatles, 9, 37–38, 181

Smart, James, 9, 111

Sonny and Cher, 129

Sounds Incorporated (group), 153

souvenirs, Beatles, 8, 45, 55, 86–91, 93–94; sent by Victor Spinetti, 9, 83, 91, 99–100, 101, 109, 111. *See also* bubblegum cards, Beatles; buttons, Beatles; dolls, Beatles

Spinetti, Victor (actor), 58, 67, 111, 153, 166, 168; awards received by, 165–66; Beatle Buddies visiting, 61–64, 67–68, 83; Beatles stories, 165, 166, 167, 169; directorial accomplishments, 166, 169; friendship with Paul, 59, 165, 171; interviews, 91, 167, 169; keeping in touch with, 180–81; letters from, 59–60, 106–7; in *Skyscraper,* 119, 121; television and theatrical roles, 97, 166. See also *Hard Day's Night, A* (movie), Victor Spinetti in [Title Index]; *Help!* (movie), Victor Spinetti in [Title Index]; *Oh What a Lovely War* (play, Raffles and Littlewood), Victor Spinetti appearing in [Title Index]

Starr, Ringo. *See* Ringo

Starr, Zak (son of Ringo), 119, 123

Stuart, Chad, 85

Sue, O.V.S.F.C.A. charter member, 64

surfing music, 82, 85

T

Taylor, Elizabeth, 166, 170

teachers. *See* nuns

Temple University, Patti attending, 153, 157–58

Tijuana Brass, 129

Tork, Peter, 149

Twinkle (singer), 92

V

Valentino, Rudolph "The Sheik," 181

Vietnam War, 151–52

Voormann, Klaus, 143

W

Ward, Burt, 130

Watts, Charlie, 92

Webber, Andrew Lloyd, 166

Welles, Orson, 166, 170

West Philadelphia Catholic High School for Girls: after-school detention, 22–23, 31, 35; Beatlemania spreading through, 21–22; graduation, 153–56; Rosary Club attends 1964 World's Fair, 36. *See also* nuns

Williams, Robert J. (critic), 28, 56

Wilson, Dennis, 85, 149

Windsor, Barbara, 62

Winters, Shelley, in *Alfie,* 149

Wyman, Bill, 130

Z

Zeffirelli, Franco, 166

TITLE INDEX

All song and album titles are attributed to the Beatles unless otherwise specified.